Windows 11
for Beginners and Seniors
2nd Edition

A Visual Guide to Learn How to Use Your New PC
with Large Text and Illustrated Instructions

ARCHER FOX

Dear Reader,

Welcome to the second edition of Windows 11 for Beginners and Seniors. This book has been carefully updated and refined to provide an even more enjoyable and effective learning experience. I've listened to your feedback, addressed common questions and concerns, and added numerous enhancements to help make using Windows 11 easier and more intuitive. My goal is to make this guide the best companion for anyone starting with Windows 11, from selecting the right computer to exploring advanced customization options.

WHAT'S NEW IN THIS 2ND EDITION?

This second edition introduces several important updates based on reader feedback and expands on key areas to enhance your learning experience:

- **Thoroughly Reviewed and Updated Content:** All chapters have been refined for better clarity and ease of use.

- **More Detailed Explanations:** Step-by-step instructions are now even more accessible, even for complete beginners.

- **How to Transfer Data from an Old PC:** A step-by-step guide for seamless data migration.

- **Enhanced Visual Aids:** Additional illustrations guide you through each process.

- **Covered Accessibility Features:** Detailed instructions on Windows 11's accessibility tools.

- **Covers More Advanced Features:** Learn beyond the basics with more in-depth coverage of advanced Windows 11 tools.
- **Optimization Recommendations:** Tips for improving performance and managing system resources.
- **More Security Features:** Including password managers, two-factor authentication, and data protection tips.

Whether you're setting up a new PC or upgrading from an older version, this edition is designed to guide you every step of the way.

WHO IS THIS BOOK FOR?

This book is intended for beginners and seniors who are new to using Windows 11 or who may feel intimidated by technology. It's perfect for anyone setting up their first computer, as well as those who want to become more comfortable and proficient with their PC. I understand that using a new computer can be daunting, especially if you're not familiar with the latest technology. This guide is here to make that process easier, breaking down complex concepts into simple, straightforward terms.

Whether you're using a computer for everyday tasks like browsing the internet and sending emails, or you're interested in personalizing your device to better suit your needs, this book will help you navigate Windows 11 with confidence. The large text and numerous illustrations are designed to make reading and following instructions as easy as possible. Even if you've had some experience with older versions of Windows, this guide will show you the new features and enhancements that make Windows 11 unique.

CONTENTS

INTRODUCTION

When Microsoft released Windows 11, I was excited to explore the new features and design. But I also worried about how my older relatives, who aren't very tech-savvy, would adapt to this new system. I realized that switching to Windows 11 could be a big challenge for them. This inspired me to create a guide, not just for my loved ones, but for all seniors who want to master this new operating system. That's how "Windows 11 for Seniors and Beginners" was born.

WHAT PROBLEMS DOES THIS BOOK SOLVE?

Problem 1: Fear of the Unknown

My parents and grandfather have used computers for years, but only for basic tasks. The idea of transitioning to Windows 11 felt overwhelming to them. They were worried they wouldn't be able to use their favorite apps and features anymore. This fear is common among many older people. In this book, I aim to build confidence, showing that Windows 11 isn't something to fear, but a step forward in technology that they can easily manage.

Problem 2: Navigating the Windows 11 Interface

I've focused on the essentials of Windows 11, such as starting the computer, using the new Start menu, and finding applications and files. The instructions are simple and straightforward, using familiar examples and plain language. I've included plenty of illustrations and screenshots so you can easily follow along.

Problem 3: Staying Connected

One of my main goals in writing this book was to help older people stay connected with family and friends. In this book, I explain how to use email, social networks, and video calling apps. I want to show that these tools can bring joy by keeping you connected with your loved ones.

Problem 4: Personalizing Your Experience

This book also guides you in customizing Windows 11 to fit your preferences. I cover how to change the display and sound settings and how to make the system easier to see and hear. My goal is to help you make your computer as comfortable and user-friendly as possible.

Problem 5: Protection and Security

I've placed special emphasis on security. Older people are often targets of online scams, so I've included a section on protecting your personal data, keeping your passwords safe, and avoiding malware. My aim is to teach you the basics of staying safe online.

Problem 6: Accessing Essential Apps

Windows 11 comes with several built-in apps that are essential for everyday tasks. In this book, I provide easy-to-follow guides on how to use these apps, whether it's browsing the web, managing your calendar, or staying in touch with loved ones. Understanding these essential apps will make your experience with Windows 11 much smoother.

Problem 7: Accessibility Features

Finally, I've made sure to include a detailed guide on the accessibility features in Windows 11. These features can help make the computer easier to use, especially for those with visual or hearing challenges. Whether it's enlarging the text or adjusting the sound, this book will show you how to customize Windows 11 to suit your needs.

Afterword: More Than Just a Book

This book isn't just a set of instructions; it's my way of showing care for the older generation. I want you to feel confident in this digital world, knowing that you can always find support and help. I believe this book will help you not only master new technologies but also discover new opportunities for communication and personal growth.

Chapter 1

GETTING STARTED WITH WINDOWS 11

1.1 UNDERSTANDING THE BASICS: PC VS. LAPTOP

In today's world, computers are an essential part of our lives. Whether you're looking up recipes, chatting with family, or watching your favorite shows, computers make it all possible. But not all computers are the same. The two main types you'll come across are PCs (personal computers) and laptops. Let's explore what makes them different and which might be best for you.

PCs: Your Home Powerhouse

A PC, or personal computer, is like the strong, reliable workhorse you can depend on at home or in the office. It's designed to handle a wide range of tasks, from simple browsing to complex operations, making it a versatile choice for many users.

One of the standout features of a PC is its **monitor**, which is usually much larger than the screen on a laptop. This makes it perfect for activities that benefit from a bigger display, such as watching movies, editing photos or videos, and even just browsing the web. The most popular monitor sizes are 24 inches and 27 inches, offering a comfortable viewing experience without taking up too much space on your desk. And the best part is, you're not locked into using a specific monitor; you can choose the one that best suits your needs and preferences.

The **system tower**, also known as the **computer case** or simply the **tower**, is the main body of your PC. It contains all the essential components that make your computer run. System towers can vary greatly in size, performance, and power consumption. Some are compact and energy-efficient, while others are larger and built for high-performance tasks. You can purchase a system tower that's already fully assembled and ready to use, or, if you prefer, you can build your own, selecting each component to match your specific needs and preferences. However, it's important to note that everything for a PC is typically bought separately. This includes the monitor, keyboard, mouse, and other peripherals like external webcams, microphones, and speakers, which you'll need to connect to your PC depending on your specific needs.

The **keyboard and mouse** allow you to interact with the computer, and with a PC, you have the freedom to choose from a wide range of options. Whether you prefer a mechanical keyboard for its tactile feedback or an ergonomic mouse that reduces strain on your wrist, you can find the perfect setup for your needs.

In summary, a PC is an excellent choice if you need a powerful and customizable computer that can handle a wide range of tasks. It offers the flexibility to choose and upgrade components, making it a strong and reliable home or office companion. Just keep in mind that with all this flexibility comes the need to purchase and connect additional equipment separately.

Laptops: Your Portable Partner

A laptop is like a mini version of a PC that you can take anywhere. It's compact, with everything built into one device, making it a highly convenient option for users who need mobility.

In a laptop, all the essential components are housed within a single chassis. This includes the display, keyboard, touchpad (which functions as a mouse), speakers, webcam, and microphone. This all-in-one design means you don't have to worry about buying and connecting separate peripherals; it's ready to use right out of the box. Whether you're at a coffee shop, in the park, or traveling, a laptop lets you work or play on the go.

Laptops are great for everyday tasks like browsing the web, writing emails, watching videos, and even light gaming. However, because everything is packed into a compact form, laptops are generally less powerful than PCs. They're designed to be energy-efficient to maintain battery life, which also means they might not handle very complex tasks as well as a PC. Additionally, powerful laptops often have shorter battery life because they use more energy.

In conclusion, a laptop is a fantastic option if you value portability and convenience. It's an all-in-one solution that's perfect for on-the-go use, though it may not offer the same power and customization options as a PC.

Which one is better?

It's clear that if you need the most powerful machine, a **PC** is generally the better choice. However, as we've discussed, both PCs and laptops can be equipped with midrange components that make them equally capable for everyday tasks like browsing the web, working on documents, or watching videos. When comparing a PC and a laptop with similar capabilities, the decision really comes down to your personal needs and how you plan to use the computer.

There are also several hidden advantages and disadvantages to consider with each type. For example, while a laptop is designed for portability, it can also be connected to external monitors, keyboards, mice, and other peripherals, giving you the flexibility to use it like a desktop when you're at home or in the office. This makes laptops versatile, allowing you to have both a portable and a more stationary setup when needed.

On the other hand, a **PC** offers a different kind of flexibility. Because each component, such as the monitor, keyboard, and mouse, is a separate product, a PC can be more future-proof. As technology advances or your needs change, you can upgrade individual parts rather than replacing the entire system. For instance, you might decide to keep your current monitor and keyboard even if you upgrade to a more powerful system tower. This ability to reuse and upgrade components over time can make a PC a more cost-effective and sustainable choice in the long run.

In the end, the choice between a PC and a laptop should be based on what you value most: portability and all-in-one convenience with a laptop, or the power, flexibility, and upgradability of a PC. Think about your daily routines and future needs to determine which option is the best fit for you.

1.2 USING THE TOUCHPAD AND MOUSE

To operate a computer, you need some kind of pointing device to interact with the interface. On smartphones and tablets, this role is played by your finger, as these devices are designed with touch in mind. While some monitors for Windows 11 computers do include touchscreen capabilities, the Windows interface isn't primarily optimized for finger use. Instead, there are two main options for navigating and controlling your computer: the **mouse** and the **touchpad**.

What's the Difference Between a Touchpad and a Mouse?

A **touchpad** is a flat, touch-sensitive surface typically found on laptops. It allows you to control the cursor by moving your fingers across it. On the other hand, a **mouse** is a separate device that you move across a flat surface to control the cursor on your screen. Each has its own advantages: a mouse generally offers more precise control, while a touchpad is compact and seamlessly integrated into the laptop, making it ideal for on-the-go use.

Types of Mice

There are various types of mice available, primarily categorized into wired and wireless options:

- **Wired Mice:** These connect directly to your computer through a USB port, providing a stable and reliable connection.
- **Wireless Mice:** These use Bluetooth or radio frequency to connect, offering greater freedom of movement without the constraint of a cable. Some wireless mice also come with additional buttons that can be customized for specific tasks, enhancing your productivity.

Using a Mouse or Touchpad: The Basics

Whether you're using a mouse or a touchpad, understanding how to control your computer effectively is key to making the most out of your experience with Windows 11. Both devices allow you to move the cursor, select items, and interact with applications, but they do so in slightly different ways. Here's a guide on how to use them, along with some practical examples.

Clicking and Selecting

- **Left Click (Mouse) / Single Tap (Touchpad):** The left click on a mouse or a single tap on a touchpad is used to select an item or open an application. For example, if you want to open your email, move the cursor over the email icon and left-click or tap once to open it.

- **Right Click (Mouse) / Two-Finger Tap (Touchpad):** The right click on a mouse or a two-finger tap on a touchpad brings up a context menu. This menu offers additional options depending on where you click. For instance, if you right-click on a photo, you might see options to copy, delete, or set it as your desktop background.

Scrolling Through Pages

- **Scroll Wheel (Mouse) / Two-Finger Scroll (Touchpad):** To move up and down through a webpage or document, you can use the scroll wheel on a mouse or slide two fingers up or down on a touchpad. This is handy when reading an article online or browsing through a long document. For example, if you're reading the news, simply scroll down to continue reading the full story.

Switching Between Applications

- **Alt + Tab (Both) / Three-Finger Swipe (Touchpad):** If you have multiple applications open, you can quickly switch between them. On a touchpad, a three-finger swipe upward will show all your open applications, allowing you to choose the one you want to switch to. On both a mouse and a touchpad, you can also use the keyboard shortcut **Alt + Tab** to cycle through your open programs. For example, if you're writing a letter in Word and want to quickly check your email, you can use these gestures to switch back and forth smoothly.

Dragging and Dropping

- **Click and Hold (Mouse) / Tap and Hold (Touchpad):** To move an item from one place to another, like dragging a file into a folder, click and hold the left mouse button while moving the mouse, or tap and hold with one finger on the touchpad while dragging your finger across it. Once the item is in the desired spot, release the button or lift your finger to drop it. For example, if you want to organize your desktop, you can drag and drop icons into different folders.

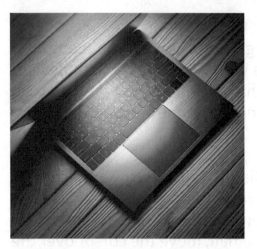

Zooming In and Out

- **Ctrl + Scroll Wheel (Mouse) / Pinch Gesture (Touch-pad):** If you need to zoom in on a webpage or document to make the text larger, hold down the **Ctrl** key and scroll up with the mouse wheel, or use a pinch gesture on the touchpad by moving two fingers apart to zoom in. To zoom out, scroll down with the mouse or pinch your fingers together on the touchpad. This is especially useful when viewing photos or reading text that might be too small.

How to Connect a Mouse to Your PC

Connecting a mouse to your computer is a straightforward process, and depending on the type of mouse you have, there are a few different methods you can use. Let's walk through each one:

1. Connecting a Wired Mouse

The process of connecting a wired mouse is very similar to connecting any other USB device, such as a flash drive, phone cable, or printer. Here's how to do it:

1. Locate an available USB port on your computer. These ports are usually found on the sides of laptops or the front and back of desktop towers.
2. Take the USB cable from your wired mouse and plug it into the USB port.
3. Once connected, your computer should automatically recognize the mouse, and it will be ready to use immediately.

This simple plug-and-play process makes using a wired mouse incredibly easy and reliable.

2. Connecting a Bluetooth Mouse

If you have a Bluetooth mouse, connecting it involves a few more steps but is still quite simple. Here's how to pair your Bluetooth mouse with a Windows 11 computer:

1. **Turn on the Bluetooth mouse** and make sure it's in pairing mode. This usually involves pressing and holding a button on the mouse until a light starts flashing.
2. **On your computer**, click on the Start menu and go to **Settings**.
3. In the Settings menu, select **Bluetooth & devices**.
4. Click on Add device at the top of the Bluetooth & devices screen.
5. In the **Add a device** window, select **Bluetooth**.
6. Your computer will start searching for available Bluetooth devices. When you see your mouse appear in the list, click on it to start the pairing process.
7. Once connected, your mouse will be ready to use wirelessly.

Bluetooth mice are great for reducing cable clutter and allowing more freedom of movement.

3. Connecting a Radio Frequency (RF) Mouse

A radio frequency (RF) mouse is another wireless option, which connects to your computer using a small USB dongle. Here's how to set it up:

1. **Locate the USB dongle** that came with your RF mouse. This is usually stored inside the mouse or in the packaging.
2. **Plug the USB dongle** into an available USB port on your computer.
3. **Turn on the mouse** using the power switch, typically located on the underside of the mouse.
4. Your computer should automatically recognize the RF mouse, and it will be ready to use.

RF mice are known for their ease of setup and strong, reliable connection without the need for Bluetooth.

Quick Guide to USB Ports on PCs and Laptops

Understanding which USB port to use can make your computing easier and more efficient. Here's a quick breakdown:

USB 2.0: Slower, best for basic devices like a mouse or keyboard. Often black inside.

USB 3.0/3.1: Faster, ideal for transferring large files to external drives. Usually blue inside.

USB-C: The newer, reversible, oval-shaped port. Great for both high-speed data and charging devices.

Pro Tip: For simple tasks, USB 2.0 works fine. For faster data transfer or charging, go with USB 3.0/3.1 or USB-C.

1.3 INTRODUCTION TO THE KEYBOARD

Using a computer keyboard in Windows 11 might seem a bit overwhelming at first, but don't worry— we'll walk through it together. Soon, you'll feel right at home with your keyboard.

Keyboard Areas

A keyboard is divided into several key areas, each serving a specific purpose:

(1) **Letter Area:** This is the main part of the keyboard where you'll find all the letters arranged in the familiar QWERTY layout, just like on a typewriter.

(2) **Number Area:** Located on the right side of the keyboard, this area includes numbers and mathematical symbols, much like a calculator. It's especially handy for quickly entering numbers.

Certain keys have special functions that can make navigating your computer easier:

(1) **Ctrl, Alt, and Shift:** These are modifier keys that change the function of other keys when pressed together. For example, pressing **Ctrl** while clicking a link often opens it in a new tab.

(2) **Windows Key:** This key opens the Start menu, giving you quick access to settings, applications, and more.

(3) **Enter:** The Enter key is used to confirm actions, such as sending an email or selecting an option in a dialog box.

(4) **Backspace:** This key allows you to delete characters you've already typed, helping you quickly correct mistakes.

(5) **F1-F12:** These function keys at the top of your keyboard perform specific actions depending on the application you're using. For instance, **F1** often opens help menus.

The Power of Keyboard Shortcuts

In addition to typing, the keyboard can be used to perform many other functions in Windows 11 and specific applications. These functions are often accessed through keyboard shortcuts—combinations of keys that, when pressed together, execute specific commands instantly. Learning a few common shortcuts can make using your computer more efficient and enjoyable.

Here are some of the most common keyboard shortcuts:

1. **Ctrl + C (Copy):** This shortcut allows you to copy selected text or files to the clipboard. For example, if you highlight a sentence in an email, pressing **Ctrl + C** will copy that sentence so you can paste it elsewhere.

2. **Ctrl + V (Paste):** After copying something with **Ctrl + C**, use **Ctrl + V** to paste it into a new location. For instance, after copying a sentence from an email, place the cursor in a document and press **Ctrl + V** to insert the text.

3. **Ctrl + Z (Undo):** Made a mistake? Press **Ctrl + Z** to undo your last action. Whether you accidentally deleted some text or moved a file to the wrong folder, **Ctrl + Z** can quickly reverse it.

4. **Ctrl + S (Save):** When working on a document or project, pressing **Ctrl + S** saves your progress. It's a good habit to save your work frequently to avoid losing it.

5. **Alt + Tab (Switch between applications):** If you have multiple applications open, **Alt + Tab** lets you quickly switch between them. For example, if you're writing a document and want to check your email, hold **Alt** and press **Tab** to toggle between your open programs.

6. **Windows Key + D (Show desktop):** This shortcut minimizes all open windows and shows the desktop. It's a quick way to access icons or files on your desktop without closing any applications.

7. **Ctrl + P (Print):** Need to print a document? **Ctrl + P** opens the print dialog box, making it easy to select your printer and print settings.

Tips for Using a Keyboard

Getting comfortable with a keyboard is an essential step in becoming confident with your computer. Here are some practical tips tailored for beginners and seniors to help you get started:

(1) **Understand Keyboard Layouts:** While all keyboards have the same basic letter area, layouts can vary depending on the model. Some keyboards include a number pad (numpad) on the right side, while others might omit it for a more compact design. You might also find keyboards without arrow keys or the F-row (function keys at the top). These variations are known as different keyboard layouts, such as **100%, TKL (Ten-keyless), 75%, 65%,** and **60%.** For ease of use, especially for beginners, I recommend choosing a keyboard with a layout between **100%, TKL, 75%,** as these will still have most of the keys you need.

(2) **Memorize the Letter Area:** The layout of the letter area on the keyboard is always the same, no matter which keyboard you use. This is the area where you'll spend most of your time typing, so it's important to familiarize yourself with where each letter is located. The more you use the keyboard, the easier it will be to remember where the keys are, making typing faster and more comfortable.

(3) **Start with Basic Navigation:** Don't worry about memorizing every Windows 11 hotkey or shortcut right away. Start by navigating your computer with the mouse to understand how things work. As you become more comfortable, you'll notice which functions you use most often, like switching between apps, copying and pasting text, or undoing mistakes. Once you're familiar with these actions, you can begin learning the shortcuts for them. For example, **Alt + Tab** to switch between applications, **Ctrl + C** to copy, and **Ctrl + V** to paste.

You've now covered the essential basics of using your computer, whether it's a PC or a laptop. You've learned about the differences between these devices, how to use the mouse, touchpad, and keyboard, and the importance of understanding keyboard layouts and shortcuts.

Chapter 2

FIRST SETUP

Setting up Windows 11 for the first time might seem daunting, but with this step-by-step guide, your computer will be up and running quickly. Before moving forward, take a moment to ensure that everything is connected correctly, especially if you're using a PC. Double-check that your monitor is correctly plugged in. PCs often have multiple monitor ports on the back of the system tower, and if your computer has a discrete GPU (graphics card), make sure the monitor is connected to the GPU's port for the best performance.

1. Power On and Plug-In

Begin by turning on your computer. Ensure it's plugged in, especially if you're setting up a laptop, to avoid interruptions during the process.

2. Choose Your Location and Language

Windows 11 will prompt you to select your country or region when you first boot up. Pick your location from the list, then choose your preferred language and keyboard layout. Click "Yes" to proceed.

3. Accept the Terms and Conditions

You'll be asked to review and accept Microsoft's Terms and Conditions. While it's always good to be informed, most users simply accept to move forward.

4. Connect to the Internet

Next, connect to your wireless network by selecting your Wi-Fi and entering the password. If you're using an Ethernet cable, your connection will be automatic.

5. Name Your Device

Windows will then prompt you to name your device. You can choose a name that reflects how you'll use the computer, such as "Office PC" or "John's Laptop." If unsure, you can skip this step and name it later.

6. Set Up for Personal Use

When asked how you'll use the device, select "Set up for personal use." This is the standard option for most users who aren't setting up their computer for work or school.

7. Sign in to Your Microsoft Account

Sign in with your Microsoft account, or create one if you don't have it. This account will sync your settings, files, and apps across devices, making it easier to manage your digital life.

8. Create a PIN

To secure your device, you'll be prompted to create a PIN. This PIN is a quick and easy way to sign in to your computer.

9. Customize Your Settings

You can customize your privacy settings, set up Windows Hello (facial recognition or finger-print), and choose additional preferences. Adjust these settings to your liking, but remember you can change them later in Settings.

10. Final Steps

Windows 11 will now finish setting up your computer, installing updates, and configuring your settings. Once complete, you'll be ready to start using your new Windows 11 device.

2.1 TRANSFERRING DATA FROM YOUR OLD PC

Transferring data from your old PC to your new Windows 11 device is crucial to ensure you have all your essential files, photos, and settings. Here's a simple guide to help you do it:

1. Use OneDrive for Cloud Transfer

One of the easiest ways to transfer data is using **OneDrive**, Microsoft's cloud storage service. Here's how:

① **Upload Files to OneDrive:** Sign in to OneDrive with your Microsoft account and upload your files and folders on your old PC. You can either drag and drop files into the OneDrive folder on your PC or use the web interface.

② **Sync on New PC:** On your new Windows 11 PC, sign in with the same Microsoft account. Your files will automatically sync to your new device, making them available immediately.

This method is ideal for moving documents, photos, and smaller files.

2. Transfer via External Storage

If you prefer not to use cloud storage or have larger files, you can transfer data using an external hard drive or USB flash drive:

① **Copy Files to External Storage:** Plug an external hard drive or USB drive into your old PC. Copy the files and folders you want to transfer to the drive.

② **Connect to New PC:** After copying the data, safely eject the drive from your old PC and plug it into your new Windows 11 PC. Then, copy the files from the drive to your new device.

This method is straightforward and doesn't require an internet connection.

3. Use a Network Transfer

If both your old and new PCs are connected to the same Wi-Fi network, you can transfer files directly between them:

Enable File Sharing: On your old PC, enable file sharing by right-clicking on the folder you want to share, selecting "Properties," then "Sharing," and following the prompts to share the folder over your network.

Access Shared Files on New PC: On your new PC, open "File Explorer," go to the "Network" section, and find your old PC. You should see the shared folders, which you can then copy to your new device.

Network transfer is useful for moving large amounts of data without needing external devices.

4. Use Windows Backup and Restore

If you're moving to a new PC from another Windows machine, you can use the built-in **Backup and Restore** feature:

① **Backup on Old PC:** On your old PC, go to "Control Panel" > "Backup and Restore" and create a backup of your files onto an external drive.

(2) **Restore on New PC:** On your new Windows 11 PC, connect the external drive and use the "Restore" feature in "Control Panel" > "Backup and Restore" to transfer your files and settings.

This method helps transfer not just files, but also some system settings and preferences.

Chapter 3

INTRODUCTION TO THE WINDOWS INTERFACE

3.1 INTRODUCTION TO THE WELCOME SCREEN

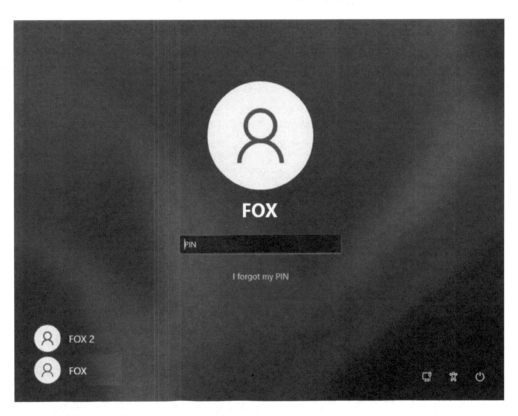

The welcome screen is the first screen that appears after starting the computer. You can see a beautiful background image, time, and date on it. This screen also has a field where you can enter your password or PIN to log in to your account.

How to use the Welcome Screen?

(1) **Viewing the screen.** First, you can just look at the beautiful background image and check the time and date.

(2) **System login.** Press any key or click the mouse. A field for entering a password or PIN will appear.

3. **Entering the password or PIN code.** Enter the password or PIN code you created when setting up your computer.

4. **Desktop access.** After entering your password or PIN code, press "Enter" or click "→", and you will be taken to the Windows 11 Desktop.

Tips for better usability

You can recover or change your password on the welcome screen if you have forgotten it.

You can customize the welcome screen background image in Windows settings.

If you don't want to enter a password, you can set up a login without a password or use the option to log in with a fingerprint or face recognition if your computer supports it.

3.2 INTRODUCTION TO THE DESKTOP

Welcome to Windows 11. This section is designed for users who are new to this operating system. Our objective is to provide you with a clear and straightforward introduction, ensuring that you become familiar with the Windows 11 desktop environment in a comfortable and understandable way.

Desktop layout

1. **Desktop.** It is the first thing you see after logging in. It looks like a real table where you put everything you need. On the Desktop, you will find icons (small images) representing shortcuts to different apps, files, or folders. You can place icons anywhere on the Desktop. They give fast access to apps, files, or folders.

(2) **Taskbar.** A long horizontal bar called the taskbar is at the bottom of the screen. You can see the icons of frequently used apps on it, allowing you to open and switch between them quickly.

(3) **Start menu.** The "Start" menu icon with the Windows logo is in the center of the taskbar. Clicking on this icon opens a menu listing all applications and system settings.

3.3 WINDOWS 11 DESKTOP ICONS

Welcome to Windows 11. This section is designed for users who are new to this operating system. Our objective is to provide you with a clear and straightforward introduction, ensuring that you become familiar with the Windows 11 desktop environment in a comfortable and understandable way.

Windows 11 Desktop icons are your virtual assistants. They help you quickly find and open apps and files.

General info about Windows 11 application icons

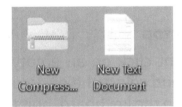  

Icons are small images representing applications, files, or folders on the Desktop. Each icon looks differently, helping to easily find the desired application or document.

How to open an application

To open the app, double-click its icon on the Desktop with the left mouse button or touchpad.

How to move icons on the Desktop

To move an icon, click it with the left mouse button on the Desktop or touchpad, hold and drag it to a new location on the Desktop.

How to rename a file on the Desktop

(1) Click the icon with the right mouse button.

(2) Select "Show more options".

(3) Select "Rename".

(4) Type a new name and press "Enter".

21

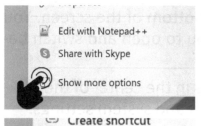

How to delete an icon on the Desktop

(1) Click an icon with the right mouse button.

(2) Select "Show more options".

(3) Select "Delete"

(4) Remember that deleting the icon doesn't delete the application itself.

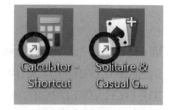

How an application icon and a shortcut differ

- Application icon gives the direct access to an application.
- Shortcut is a link leading to an application, file, or folder stored elsewhere on your computer.

You can distinguish them by an arrow on the application icon.

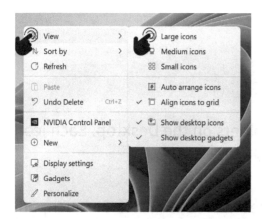

How to scale up icons on the Desktop

To increase the size of the icons, right-click on an empty space on the desktop, select "View" and select the desired icon size. Or hold down the CTRL key on the keyboard, point the mouse anywhere on the desktop, and scroll the mouse wheel up or down to increase or decrease the size of the icons, respectively.

Interaction with desktop icons using the right mouse button

Right-clicking on the icon opens a context menu where you can select various options such as open, rename, delete or view properties. To open all available menu options, click "Show more options".

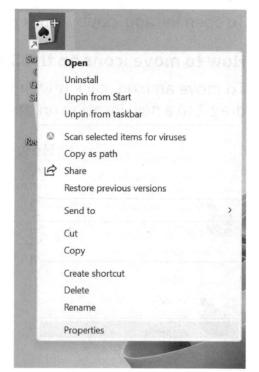

3.4 HOW TO CREATE A FOLDER ON WINDOWS 11 DESKTOP

In this section, we'll take a closer look at what a Windows 11 folder is and how you can create, name, and use folders to organize your files and icons. This guide is intended for seniors who are getting to know a computer for the first time.

What is a folder?

The Windows 11 folder is like a real folder, but only on your computer. It helps you virtually organize your files (documents, photos, videos, etc.). You can create as many folders as you like and sort files by topic or category, just like you would put papers in a real folder.

How to create a folder on the Desktop

1. **Go to the Desktop.** Make sure you are on the Desktop. That is what you see after logging in to your computer account or when you close all application windows.
2. **Create a new folder.** Right-click on an empty space on the Desktop (not on icons). In the context menu, select "New" and then "Folder".

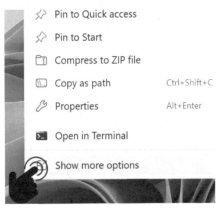

How to name a folder on the Desktop

1. **Default name.** Your new folder will initially be named "New folder". It is the default name.
2. **Rename a folder.** To change the name of a folder, right-click on the "New folder" icon, select "**Show more options**" and then "**Rename**". Type the desired name and press "Enter" on the keyboard.

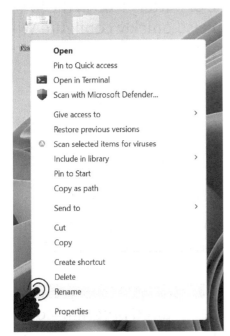

How to move files or icons into a folder

1. **Select a file or icon.** Find a file or icon you want to move into a folder. These may be a document, photo, application shortcut, etc.
2. **Move a file/icon.** Left-click on the file or icon and, holding the button, drag it to the folder icon. When the folder is selected, release the mouse button.

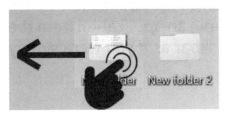

Folders are an excellent means to maintain order on the Desktop. You can create folders for different file categories, such as photos, documents, music, or specific projects. This can help you easily find a file when you need it. Don't be afraid to experiment and create as many folders as you need for comfortable work on your computer.

3.5 INTRODUCTION TO WINDOWS 11 TASKBAR

The **Taskbar** is one of the main elements of Windows 11, which plays a key role in interaction with the computer.

General info about Windows 11 Taskbar

The taskbar is a long horizontal bar usually located at the bottom of your screen. You can find application icons, the notification center, and quick access buttons for various system functions on it.

Taskbar icons

The icons of the most frequently used applications are usually located on the Taskbar. These are your browser, mail client, music player, etc. By clicking on the icon, you can quickly open the necessary application.

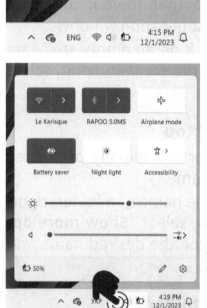

The right side of the Taskbar

The Notification Center and Quick Settings are on the right side of the Taskbar. There you can see the time, date, internet connection status, battery charge (for laptops) and other system icons.

Quick Settings

To open it, click on the Internet, volume or battery icon in the lower right corner of the Taskbar. You can also quickly configure Wi-Fi, Bluetooth, volume and screen brightness there.

Notification Center on the Taskbar

The Notification Center is on the right side of the Taskbar. There you can see icons of system processes, such as antivirus, Windows Service Center, network indicator and others.

Application icons on the Taskbar

- **How to start an application from the Taskbar:** Left-click on the required program icon.
- **How to pin an application shortcut to the Taskbar:** Right-click on the application icon in the "**Start**" menu and select "**Pin to Taskbar**". If you need to pin an application from the Desktop, drag it with the mouse from the Desktop to the Taskbar as if you were simply moving a file on the Desktop.

- **How to delete an application shortcut from the Taskbar:** Right-click on the application icon on the Taskbar and select "**Unpin from Taskbar**".

Switching between opened applications

If you open several applications, you can easily switch between them by clicking on the corresponding icons on the Taskbar. The active application window is highlighted on the Taskbar.

"Start" menu icon and search bar

The "Start" menu icon with the Windows logo is on the left side or in the center of the Taskbar. Clicking on it opens a menu with a list of applications, settings and files. The search bar is next to the Start menu icon. You can use it to search for files, applications, and information on the Internet.

Conclusion

Windows 11 Taskbar is a powerful tool that helps you interact with your computer efficiently. You can use it to quickly launch applications, view messages, manage windows and do many other things. Learning to use the taskbar is an important step in understanding the basics of computer literacy. Feel free to experiment and use all the possibilities it offers.

3.6 INTRODUCTION TO THE WINDOWS 11 "START" MENU

The Windows 11 "**Start**" menu is a central part of your computer interaction. It provides quick access to applications, files, system settings, and other useful resources. The goal of this section is to help seniors new to Windows 11 understand and use the "Start" menu effectively.

General info about the "Start" menu

You can open the "Start" menu by clicking on the icon with the Windows logo on the left side or in the center of the Taskbar. In this menu, you can find shortcuts to access applications, files, system settings, and shut down the computer.

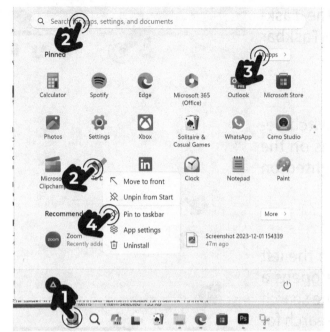

How to pin applications in the "Start" menu

1. Left-click on the icon with the Windows logo on the Taskbar.
2. Find the required application in the list of available applications, or use the search bar.
3. You can also go to "All Apps", where you can find all applications installed on your PC.
4. Right-click on the application icon and select "Pin to Start".

How to delete applications from the "Start" menu

1. Left-click on the icon with the Windows logo.
2. Find the application you need to delete.
3. Right-click on the application and select "Unpin from Start".

How to shut down, restart or put the device into sleep mode through the "Start" menu

1. Left-click on the icon with the Windows logo.
2. Left-click on the power icon (which is usually a circle with a short trace at the top).
3. Select "Shut down", "Restart" or "Sleep" as required.

26

How to open a list of all installed applications from the "Start" menu

(1) Left-click on the icon with the Windows logo.

(2) Left-click on "All apps"

(3) Scroll through the list of applications that opens in the Start menu to see all the apps installed on your computer.

How to move the "Start" menu from the center to the left corner of the Taskbar

(1) Right-click on the empty space on the Taskbar.

(2) Select "Taskbar settings".

(3) On the tab "Taskbar behaviors" find the setting "Taskbar alignment" and select the option "Left".

Conclusion

The Start menu is an integral part of Windows 11, providing you with quick access to all the resources you need. Following these step-by-step instructions, you can manage your computer's applications, files, and settings efficiently.

3.7 HOW TO WORK WITH WINDOWS

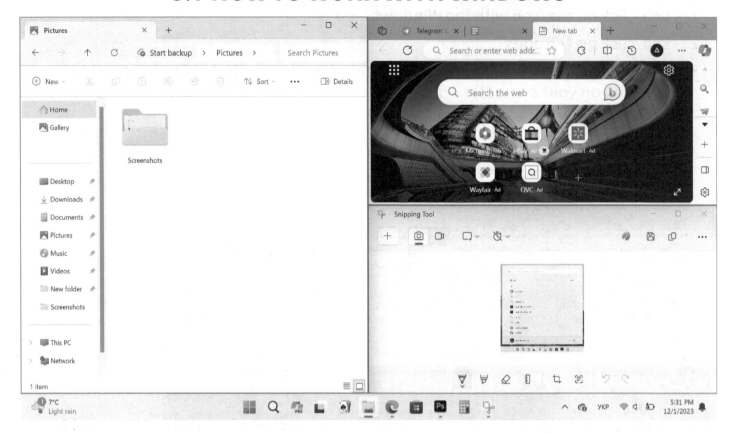

The windows are your virtual "eyes" into the world of applications and files. The windows may be different applications, documents or folders. These are like pages in a book, where each page is a separate window.

Window hierarchy

You can open several windows at the same time. The active window is the one you are currently working with. It will be on top of other windows. How to understand which window is active? See which one is highlighted.

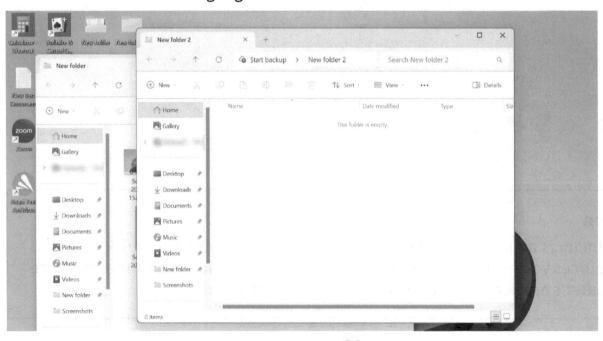

- **How to delete an application shortcut from the Task-bar:** Right-click on the application icon on the Taskbar and select "**Unpin from Taskbar**".

Switching between opened applications

If you open several applications, you can easily switch be-tween them by clicking on the corresponding icons on the Taskbar. The active application window is highlighted on the Taskbar.

"Start" menu icon and search bar

The "Start" menu icon with the Windows logo is on the left side or in the center of the Taskbar. Clicking on it opens a menu with a list of applications, settings and files. The search bar is next to the Start menu icon. You can use it to search for files, applications, and information on the Internet.

Conclusion

Windows 11 Taskbar is a powerful tool that helps you interact with your computer efficiently. You can use it to quickly launch applications, view messages, manage win-dows and do many other things. Learning to use the taskbar is an important step in understanding the basics of computer literacy. Feel free to experiment and use all the possibilities it offers.

3.6 INTRODUCTION TO THE WINDOWS 11 "START" MENU

The Windows 11 "**Start**" menu is a central part of your computer interaction. It provides quick access to applications, files, system settings, and other useful resources. The goal of this sec-tion is to help seniors new to Windows 11 understand and use the "Start" menu effectively.

General info about the "Start" menu

You can open the "Start" menu by clicking on the icon with the Windows logo on the left side or in the center of the Taskbar. In this menu, you can find shortcuts to access applications, files, system settings, and shut down the computer.

How to pin applications in the "Start" menu

1. Left-click on the icon with the Windows logo on the Taskbar.
2. Find the required application in the list of available applications, or use the search bar.
3. You can also go to "All Apps", where you can find all applications installed on your PC.
4. Right-click on the application icon and select "Pin to Start".

How to delete applications from the "Start" menu

1. Left-click on the icon with the Windows logo.
2. Find the application you need to delete.
3. Right-click on the application and select "Unpin from Start".

How to shut down, restart or put the device into sleep mode through the "Start" menu

1. Left-click on the icon with the Windows logo.
2. Left-click on the power icon (which is usually a circle with a short trace at the top).
3. Select "Shut down", "Restart" or "Sleep" as required.

26

Components of an application or folder window

Any window has these components:

1. **Title** (the name of an application or a folder)

2. **Control buttons** (minimize, maximize, and close) in the right upper corner

3. **Content area** (information about the application, or its content)

How to maximize a window

To maximize a window, left-click on the button with two diagonal arrows (or a square) in the right upper corner of the window. It's like opening a window in your apartment to full width, giving in so much air and light!

How to minimize a window

To minimize a window, left-click on a short line (or a dash) in the right upper corner of the window. The window will "hide" on the Taskbar, like a cat hiding under the sofa.

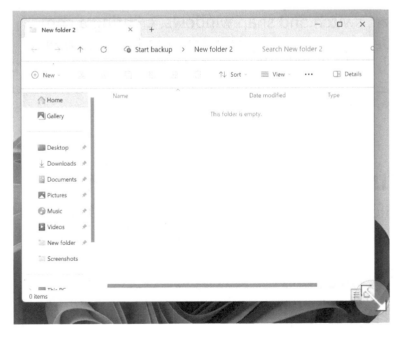

How to resize a window

To change the size of a window, move the mouse cursor to the edge of the window until it turns into arrows. Then pull the window in the right direction, as if you were pulling a blanket over yourself at night.

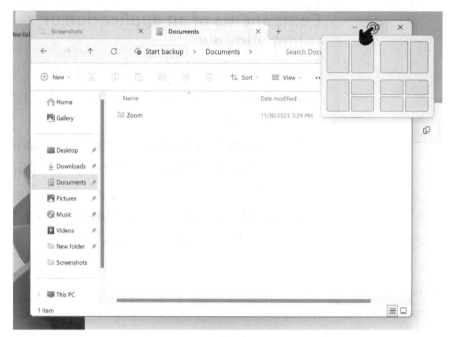

How to snap a window

Snap a window means making it visible on half or a quarter of the screen. It is convenient when you want to work with two applications at the same time. Drag the window to one of the corners of the screen and it will automatically snap. Or hover the mouse cursor over the square icon in the right upper corner of the window and select the required window location.

How to switch between windows

You can switch between windows by clicking their icons on the Taskbar. You can also use the hotkey Alt+Tab to view open windows and select the one you need.

How to snap several windows on the Desktop

To snap more than one window on the Desktop, open the required windows and snap them as described above. You can snap up to four windows on the Desktop.

Conclusion

Working with windows is not black magic, but a simple and understandable process. You can easily open, minimize, maximize, switch and snap windows, creating a comfortable working space. Remember that every time you open a new window, you open up new opportunities. Enjoy your digital world and don't hesitate to experiment!

3.8 HOW TO WORK WITH "FILE EXPLORER" IN WINDOWS 11

File Explorer is your personal archivist of files and folders on your computer. It is like a storage where every file and folder has its own place.

General info about using File Explorer in Windows 11

File Explorer is an application that helps you view, manage, and find files on your computer. It is a kind of map that tells you where each file or folder is.

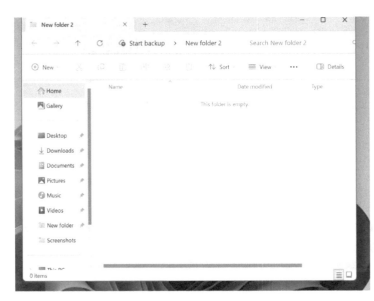

File Explorer window components

File Explorer window has several parts:

① **Quick access panel.** There you can find shortcuts for the most frequently used folders.

② **Working space.** It is the central part of the window where your files and folders are displayed.

③ **Address bar.** It is located at the top of the window and shows the path to the selected folder.

④ **Search bar.** It helps you find the files you need by typing their names and pressing "Enter".

Quick access panel overview

The Quick access panel is, like bookmarks in a book, where you save links to your favorite or frequently used folders. To add a folder, select it in the File Explorer working space and drag it to the Quick access panel, just as you earlier pinned applications to the Taskbar.

Working space overview

In the working space, you can see the contents of your folders. You can open, move, copy and delete files, like in a big archive where every document has its place.

Address bar

In File Explorer, the address bar is similar to the address on an envelope. It shows your current location in your computer's file system. You can click on any part of the path in the address bar to quickly go to another folder.

File Explorer search

To find a file, use the search bar in the right upper corner of the File Explorer window. Type the name of a file or a keyword, and File Explorer will find it for you.

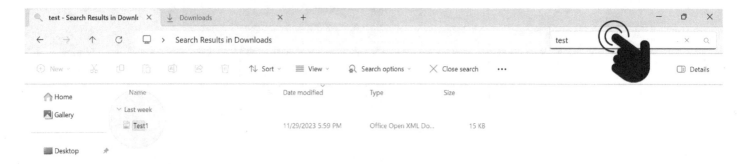

Sorting files in File Explorer

You can sort files by name, date, type and other options. To do this, right-click on any free place in the working space and select the appropriate sorting option.

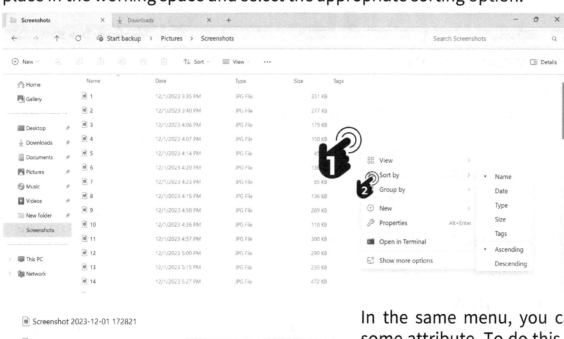

In the same menu, you can group files by some attribute. To do this, select the option "Group by".

How to resize icons in File Explorer

To change the size of icons, right-click on any empty space in File Explorer and select "View" -> "Large icons", "Extra large icons", etc.

Or, holding the CTRL key, point the cursor over the File Explorer working space, and scroll up or down with the mouse wheel.

Going to File Explorer libraries

File Explorer has special folders, such as "Downloads", "Music", "Documents", "Videos" and "Pictures". The appropriate files are automatically saved to these folders, helping you organize your data.

"This PC" folder

All the devices and disks connected to your computer are displayed in this folder. There you can see hard disks, external devices, etc.

What are storage drives

Storage drives are like big vaults where your computer keeps all your data. You can think of them as big folders where all your files are stored. Storage drive icon shows how much free space you have left on them. When this space runs out, you will no longer be able to add new files. So, make sure that the space is always enough. For this you only need to delete files you no longer use.

What is the difference between the Desktop and File Explorer

- The desktop is like the top of your real table where you put the most important things.
- File Explorer is like all the drawers and cabinets where everything else is kept.
- Desktop is for quick access, and File Explorer is for thorough organization.

Conclusion

Windows 11 File Explorer is your reliable assistant in the world of files and folders. It helps you find, organize and manage your data. Don't hesitate to use its features, because every time you open File Explorer, you open the door to your digital library!

Chapter 4

PERSONALIZATION AND CUSTOMIZATION IN WINDOWS 11

Personalizing your Windows 11 experience is more than just making things look nice—it's about making your computer work better for you. In this chapter, we'll show you how to customize different aspects of Windows 11 to suit your needs and preferences.

We'll start with accessibility features, ensuring your computer is as easy to use as possible. We'll explore how to change wallpapers, colors, themes, and more from there. By the end of this chapter, you'll know how to create a Windows environment that feels comfortable and reflects your style, making everyday tasks easier and more enjoyable.

4.1 ACCESSIBILITY FEATURES IN WINDOWS 11

Windows 11 offers a range of accessibility features designed to help users customize their experience based on individual needs. Here's how to access and use these features.

How to Access Accessibility Settings

To start, open the Start Menu and navigate to Settings. From there, select "Accessibility" on the left-hand sidebar to explore the various features available.

Vision

 Text Size allows you to adjust the text size across Windows and your apps, which is useful if you find the default text too small to read comfortably.

 Visual Effects lets you customize interface elements like scroll bars, transparency, and animations to reduce visual clutter. For example, you can choose to always show scrollbars or turn off unnecessary animations, which can make navigation clearer and faster.

 Mouse Pointer and Touch helps enhance visibility by allowing you to change the size and color of the mouse pointer, making it easier to locate on the screen, especially if you struggle to see the default pointer.

 Text Cursor offers options to modify the appearance and thickness of the text cursor, along with the ability to add a visual indicator. This feature is particularly useful if you have difficulty spotting where you're typing.

 Magnifier is a tool that enlarges parts of your screen, making it easier to see small text or detailed images. You can adjust the zoom level, set it to follow your mouse pointer, or even choose specific areas to magnify. You can quickly turn it on or off with the **Win + Plus** and **Win + Minus** keys.

 Color Filters help users with color blindness distinguish between colors by applying filters like grayscale or inverted colors. This can be essential for users who have difficulty telling certain colors apart. You can toggle this feature on or off using **Win + Ctrl + C**.

 Contrast Themes increase the contrast between text and background, making it easier to read content on the screen, especially in low-light conditions or for those with low vision. You can choose from preset high-contrast themes or create a custom one.

Narrator is a built-in screen reader that provides voice feedback, allowing users with low vision or blindness to navigate the system without needing to see the screen. You can adjust the voice speed, pitch, verbosity, and keyboard layout to suit your needs. Activate Narrator with **Win + Ctrl + Enter**.

Hearing

 Audio combines stereo sound into a single channel for users who have hearing loss in one ear. This ensures you don't miss any audio information, as all sounds are played through both speakers or headphones.

Interaction

 Captions allow you to display text captions for audio content, making it easier to follow along with videos or other media. You can customize the style, size, and color of the captions to suit your preferences.

 Speech allows you to control your computer and dictate text using voice commands, ideal for users who have difficulty using a keyboard or mouse. You can set up voice access, enable voice typing, and configure speech recognition settings. Start dictation by pressing **Win + H**.

 Keyboard settings can be adjusted to make typing easier, particularly for those with mobility issues. You can enable Sticky Keys, which lets you press keys sequentially rather than simultaneously, Filter Keys to ignore brief or repeated keystrokes, and Toggle Keys to hear a sound when certain keys are pressed. You can also use the on-screen keyboard if you have difficulty using a physical one.

 Mouse settings allow you to adjust the speed and acceleration of the mouse pointer. Additionally, you can enable mouse keys, which lets you control the pointer using the numeric keypad. This is activated with **Alt + Left Shift + Num Lock**.

 Eye Control is designed for users with severe mobility impairments, allowing them to navigate the computer using eye-tracking technology. You can set up and calibrate the eye tracker, adjust dwell time (the time your eyes need to focus on an item to select it), and customize actions for smoother interaction.

These accessibility features are designed to make Windows 11 more user-friendly and tailored to your specific needs, ensuring a comfortable and effective computing experience.

General info about Windows 11 personalization

Windows 11 personalization is adapting the look and feel of your operating system to suit your personal preferences. It may concern changing the Desktop wallpaper, the Taskbar color, system sounds and much more.

How to open Windows 11 settings panel

To start personalization, you need to open the settings panel.

① Right-click on the Desktop.

② Select **Personalize**.

This is the shortest path to all kinds of settings. It is like a key to a secret treasure chest.

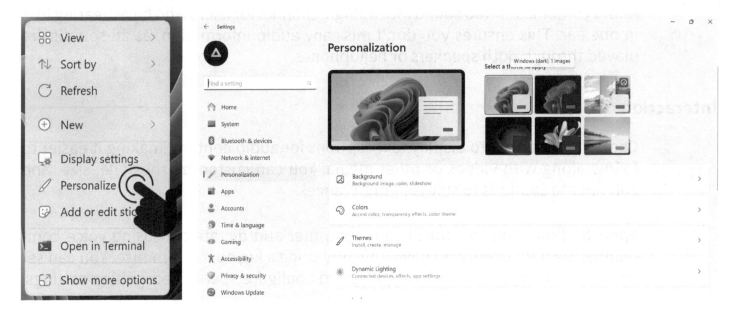

Personalization options
Wallpaper personalization:

- To change the wallpaper on the Desktop, select "Background".
- You can use your photos or standard Windows wallpapers.

Color personalization:

- On the personalization options panel, select "Colors". You can select the main color for Windows and also adjust transparency and other settings.
- You can adjust colors to match your wallpaper or suit your preferences.

Lock screen personalization:

- Like wallpapers, you can select an image or slideshow for your lock screen.
- You can also choose the information (for example time, calendar) to be displayed on the lock screen.

Interface and font size settings:

- You can make text and elements on the screen larger or smaller.
- This is useful if you need larger text for better reading or to fit more information on the screen.

4.2 WALLPAPER PERSONALIZATION IN WINDOWS 11

Your computer wallpaper is like the face of your digital friend. Creation involves destruction. So, let's destroy boredom and create something magical!

This is your chance to add a personal touch to the look of your computer. You can select an image from the large collection offered by Windows or use your own photos.

How to open the personalization panel in Windows 11

- **Opening the settings from the Desktop.** Right-click on the Desktop and select "Personalize".

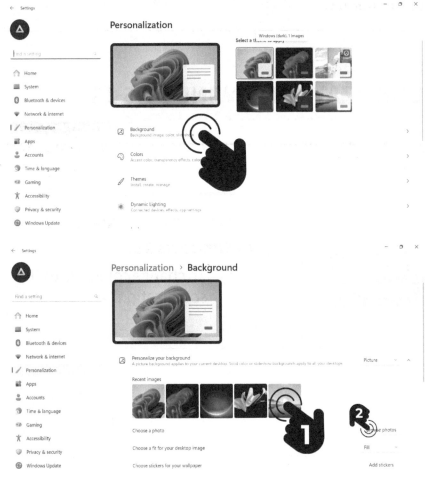

How to change the wallpaper

1. **Selection from presets.** On the "Personalization" panel, select "Background".

2. There, you will find a gallery of images offered by Windows. Choose the one you like the most.

3. **Using your photos:** If you want to use your image, left-click on "Browse photos" and select a photo on your computer. You can choose a snapshot from your last trip or a photo of your favorite pet.

Desktop background image filling options

After you've selected an image, you'll have to select the options for filling in the image:

- **Stretch.** The image will stretch to fill the whole screen.
- **Fill.** The image will fill the screen while keeping the aspect ratio.
- **Fit.** The image will fit into the screen, keeping the proportions without cutting off the edges.
- **Tile.** The image will be repeated like a tile.

Wallpaper personalization in Windows 11 is the easiest and most effective way to make your computer more personal and comfortable. It is your digital home, so let it reflect your interests, hobbies or even dreams. Remember that changing the wallpaper is not just a change of image, it is an expression of your style and mood. Enjoy every moment you start your computer, because it will greet you with the look you chose!

> *If you find that the personalization features in Windows 11 aren't active, it's possible that your Windows isn't activated. To resolve this, refer to Chapter 7.2 for step-by-step instructions on how to activate your Windows.*

4.3 COLOR PERSONALIZATION IN WINDOWS 11

Color personalization in Windows 11 is a way to change the look of your operating system by choosing a color that matches your style and mood. You can choose colors for the Start menu, window titles, Taskbar, and more.

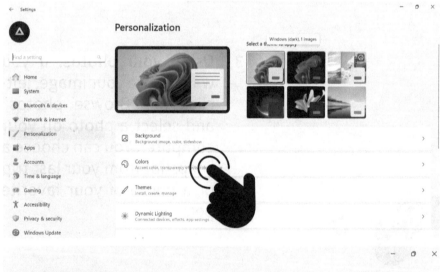

How to change colors in Windows 11

① To change colors, go to "Personalization" > "Colors".

② There you can select either the "Light" or "Dark" mode.

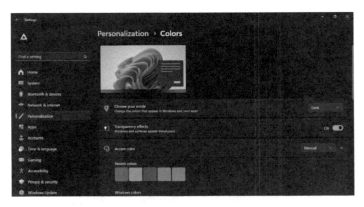

Pros of the dark mode. The mode reduces eye strain in the dark. It also looks stylish and modern.

Pros of the light mode. The mode provides better visibility in bright light. Also, it seems more traditional and familiar.

How to change the color of the "Start" menu:

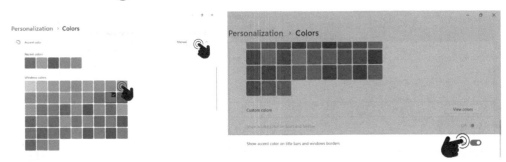

On the tab "Colors", you can also change the color of the "Start" menu and Taskbar. Or go to "Custom colors" and select the color you like.

How to change the color of title bars and window borders:

You can also change the color of title bars and window borders.

To do this, check the box next to "Show accent color on title bars and windows borders".

Color personalization in Windows 11 is not only about beauty, but also about comfort. The right color can affect your mood and productivity. Don't hesitate to experiment with different colors and modes. Remember that your computer is not just a tool, but a part of your personal space that should reflect your personality. So let your Windows 11 shine with bright colors that please your eye!

4.4 WINDOWS 11 THEMES

In Windows 11, themes are sets of visual elements that change the look of your Desktop, including the background, colors, system sounds, and mouse cursor. It's like giving your computer a new outfit! Themes are not just changing the Desktop color or background; they are a complete interface transformation. It is like adding a modern look to your classic-style living room at the touch of a button. This is how themes work in Windows 11!

How to change themes in Windows 11

(1) On the "Personalization" panel, select "Themes". And you will see a list of available themes.

(2) You can choose one of the standard Windows themes (1) or download new themes from the Microsoft Store (2).

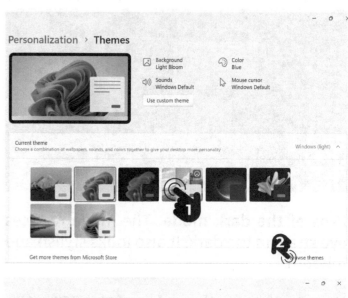

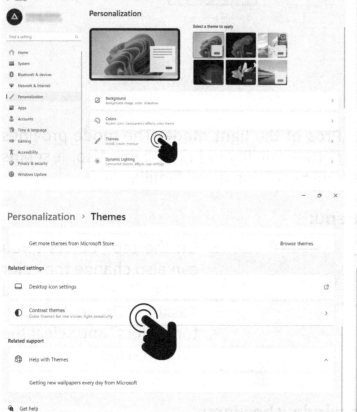

(3) Click on the theme you liked and your interface will change at once.

Contrast themes in Windows 11

You can also choose contrast themes in Windows 11. To do this:

(1) On the "Themes' panel, select "Contrast themes".

(2) Choose the most suitable for you from the options in the "Contrast themes" menu and click "Apply".

Contrast themes are helpful for people with visual impairments. You can also use them if you want interface elements to be highlighted.

4.5 TASKBAR PERSONALIZATION

The **Taskbar** is a place that contains all the essential tools for managing your computer. It gives you quick access to applications, settings, notifications, and other essential functions.

In Windows 11, the Taskbar is usually at the bottom of the screen and includes application icons, the search bar, the "Start" menu, and other useful tools. It is like a remote control for your computer!

How to customize Taskbar items

(1) Right-click on the Taskbar.

(2) Select "Taskbar settings".

You can add or remove Taskbar items, providing quick access to important functions. These are as follows:

(1) Change the look of the "Search" bar. You can select the options "Search box", "Search icon and label", or "Search icon only". You can also hide it.

(2) Enable or disable displaying the "Copilot" panel.

(3) Enable or disable displaying the "Task view" panel.

(4) Enable or disable displaying the "Widgets" panel.

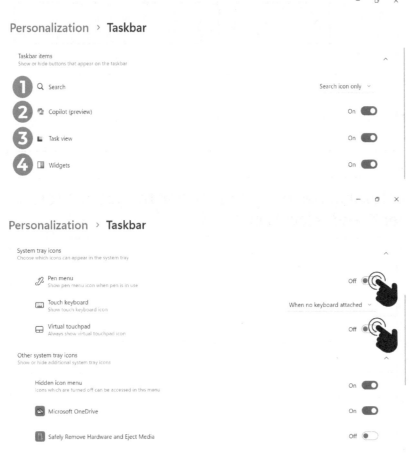

How to add or delete elements from the Taskbar

(1) To set displaying icons on the Taskbar, select "System tray icons" and "Other system tray icons".

(2) You can choose which icons to display on the Taskbar.

4.6 "START" MENU PERSONALIZATION

The "**Start**" menu is the center of Windows 11, where you can find everything you need: applications, settings, files, and more. It's like a digital Swiss army knife.

"Start" menu overview

① How to open the "Start" menu. Left-click on the icon with the Windows logo, or press the Windows key on the keyboard.

② How to open the "Start" menu settings. Right-click on the "Start" menu and select "Start settings".

How to personalize the list of applications in the "Start" menu

You can add or remove applications from the "Start" menu. To do it, right-click on an application in the "Start" menu and select "Pin" or "Unpin".

How to change the location of the "Start" menu

In the "Start" menu settings, you can change the menu size, making it larger or smaller. You can select one of 3 display options, namely:

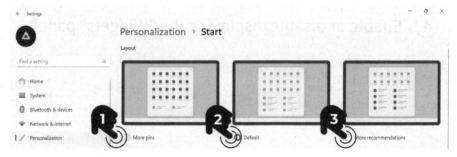

How to move the "Start" menu from the center to the left corner of the Taskbar

① Right-click on the empty space of the Taskbar and select "Taskbar settings".

② On the "Taskbar behaviors" panel, find the option "Taskbar alignment" and select "Left".

4.7 INTERFACE AND FONT SIZE SETTINGS IN WINDOWS 11

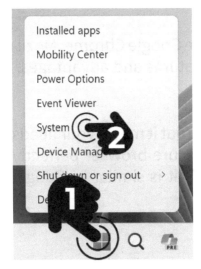

Interface scaling

1. Right-click on the icon with the Windows logo and select "Settings".

2. In the window that opens, select "System", which is the first item in the list.

3. On the "System" panel, select "Display". There you will find all the settings related to the display of your computer.

4. On the "Scale" panel, you will see a drop-down menu with scaling options.

5. Select the one that best suits your needs. These are 100%, 125%, 150% or more.

View changes

After selecting a scaling option, your display will automatically update to show the change. If you're not happy with the change, repeat the above steps and choose a different size.

Chapter 5

USING THE EDGE BROWSER AND GOING ONLINE

A browser is an application making it possible to visit web pages on the Internet. It is your File Explorer in the world of information, entertainment and knowledge, which is available right on your computer.

Why do you need a browser?

You need a browser to read news, watch videos, listen to music, shop, communicate with friends and do many other things on the Internet. It is like a magic carpet that can instantly transport you to any corner of the digital world.

What browsers do you know?

There are many different browsers, among which the most famous are Google Chrome, Mozilla Firefox, Safari, and, surely, Microsoft Edge. Each browser has its features and advantages.

Which browser is better, and why choose Edge?

 Choosing a browser is like choosing a friend: it's important that it meets your needs and desires. Microsoft Edge is an up-to-date, fast, and secure browser perfectly integrated with Windows 11. Moreover, "under the hood" it is similar to Google Chrome, so there is no need to download another browser.

Advantages of the integrated Edge browser

- **Windows integration.** Edge is integrated with Windows 11, so it seamlessly works and syncs with your settings and Microsoft account.
- **Speed and efficiency.** Edge uses fewer resources, which ensures fast operation even on older computers.
- **Security and privacy.** Microsoft is constantly working to ensure the security and privacy of Edge users.
- **Additional features.** Edge offers many useful features, such as a reading mode, an integrated translator, and the possibility of adding extensions.

5.2 NAVIGATING THE EDGE INTERFACE

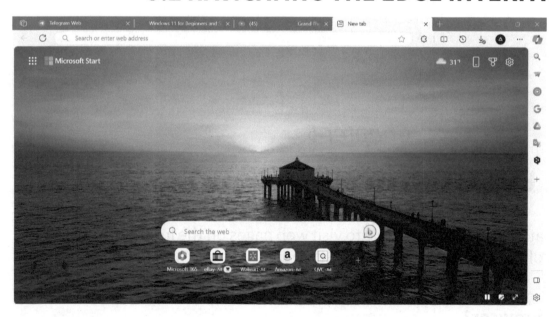

To use the Edge easily, it is important to know its basic elements. Imagine that the browser is your window to the world of the Internet, and every element of this window helps you better see and explore this world.

Address bar

The **address bar** is a long rectangle at the top of the browser window where you enter a web address (URL) or search queries. It's like a GPS for the internet, helping you pinpoint exactly where you want to go.

Click on it and type in the website address like "www.google.com" or type a search query like "weather today" and press "Enter".

Favorites

The **Favorites** is a bar under the address bar where you can "save" frequently visited web pages. It's like bookmarks in a book that help you quickly find the right place.

How to add a bookmark?

When you are on the page you want to save, click the star to the right of the address bar. Choose where to save the bookmark and click "Done".

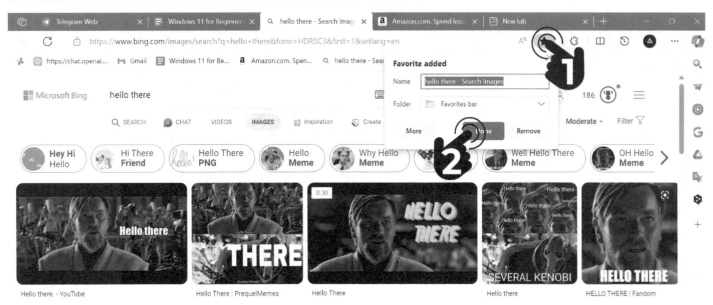

Control panel

The Control panel is a set of icons in the upper right part of the browser that gives access to various functions of the Edge, such as settings, browsing history, downloads, and more.

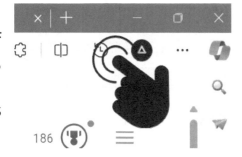

Click on the icon (for example, the three dots for the settings menu) and the appropriate menu with options will open.

Sidebar

The **Sidebar** is an additional panel on the right side of the browser window that provides quick access to the Favorites, browsing history, and other useful tools.

Click on the Sidebar icon (usually at the top right corner) to expand it and access its features.

Edge home page

The **Home page** is the first page you see when you open the Edge. You can find the search bar, quick links to websites and other useful information on it.

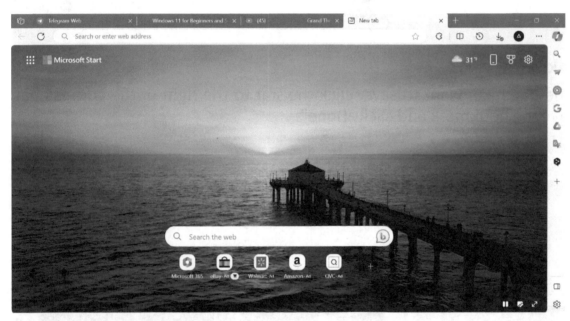

Use the Home page for quick access to the search, your favorites, and useful information.

What is a browser tab?

Imagine you are reading a book and can have several different pages opened simultaneously, each leading you to different chapters or books. In the world of the Internet, a "tab" in the Edge browser is just such a "page". Each browser tab is a separate window or section where you can open different web pages. You can open many tabs at the same time and switch between them as if you were turning the pages of a book.

How to add a tab?

It is very easy to add a new tab in the Edge browser:

1. **Find the Tab panel.** Look at the top of the browser where you'll see a row of small rectangles or "tabs" that are already open.

2. **Add a new tab.** Find and click on the small icon that looks like a plus sign ("+") usually located to the right of the last tab. A new tab will be added.

③ **Go to a new tab.** After clicking on the plus sign, a new tab will open. Now you can type in the address of the web page you want to visit in the address bar above.

How to close a tab?

It is as easy to close a tab as to open it:

① **Find the tab you want to close.** Look at the tab bar and find the required tab. The tab you are currently viewing will usually be highlighted.

② **Close the tab.** On the tab you want to close, you will see a small cross ("X") on the right side. Click on this cross and the tab will close.

The Edge is more than a browser. It is your faithful assistant in learning the endless world of the Internet. The application will help you quickly and safely learn new things, have fun, shop, communicate, and much more. Remember that it's never too late to learn something new, and the Edge is a great tool for that.

5.3 ONLINE SEARCHES AND USING GOOGLE

Imagine a world where all the information you'll ever need is just a few clicks away. And thanks to Google, the most popular search engine in the world, it is not a fantasy but a reality. Let's find out how you can use this powerful tool.

General info about the Google search engine

is not just a website, it's a huge library of knowledge. Type in any word or phrase and Google will find pages on the Internet where these words occur. It is like a magic key to endless treasures of information.

Why Google is a popular choice for web search

is speed, simplicity and accuracy. This search engine can find almost anything you're looking for in seconds. Whether it's a borscht recipe, the latest news, or how to use a new device, Google has the answer.

How to open Google via a browser

1. Open a browser (for example, the Edge) by clicking on its icon.
2. In the address bar at the top of the browser, type in "www.google.com" and press "Enter".

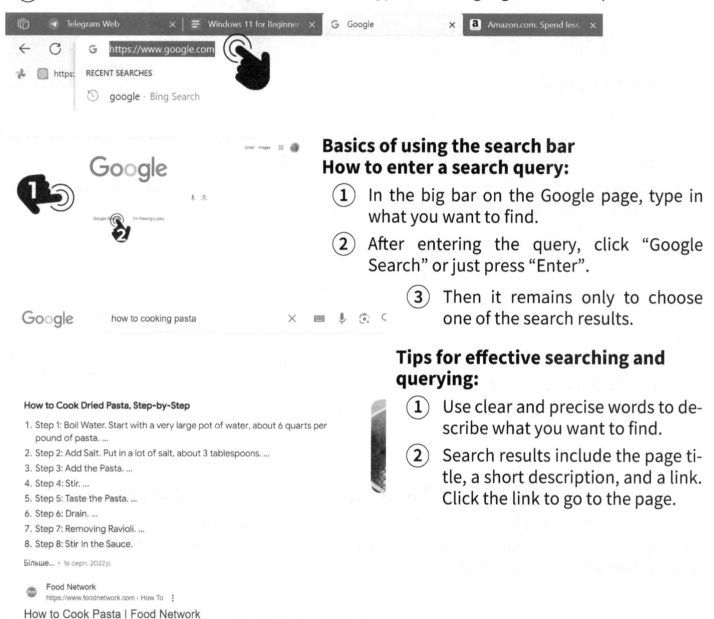

Basics of using the search bar
How to enter a search query:

1. In the big bar on the Google page, type in what you want to find.
2. After entering the query, click "Google Search" or just press "Enter".
3. Then it remains only to choose one of the search results.

Tips for effective searching and querying:

1. Use clear and precise words to describe what you want to find.
2. Search results include the page title, a short description, and a link. Click the link to go to the page.

Examples of Google search queries you can use for different purposes:

Search for recipes

Borscht recipe:
Query: "authentic Ukrainian borscht recipe"

Chocolate cake recipe:
Query: "Simple chocolate cake recipe"

Vegetarian dish recipes:
Query: "Vegetarian lunch recipes"

Order a pizza

Find pizzerias nearby:
Query: "Pizzerias nearby"

Order a pizza online:
Query: "Order pizza online in Kyiv"

Pizza with home delivery:
Query: "Pizza with home delivery in Seattle"

Search for medical instructions

Instructions for Aspirin:
Query: "aspirin instructions"

Dosage and side effects of Paracetamol:
Query: "paracetamol dosage and side effects"

Interaction of drugs:
Query: "Interaction of amoxicillin with other drugs"

These queries will help you quickly find the information you need on Google, make a choice or order, and use medicines safely.

5.4 SEARCHING FOR VIDEOS ON YOUTUBE

You Tube is a free video hosting where users can watch, download and share videos. It's like TV but you can choose what to watch and when.

Free use and Premium access

- **Free use.** On YouTube, you can watch most videos for free, but with ads.
- **Premium access.** It is a paid subscription that provides ad-free access, the option to download videos and listen to music without interruptions.

When you open YouTube, the first thing you see is the home page. It is your window to the world of incredible and diverse video content. Let's take a closer look at it.

Basic home page sections

1. **Home.** On the home page, you will find videos that YouTube thinks are interesting for you. They are selected based on your previously viewed videos and interests. These can be popular videos, new videos from channels you are subscribed to, or videos from your preferred topics.

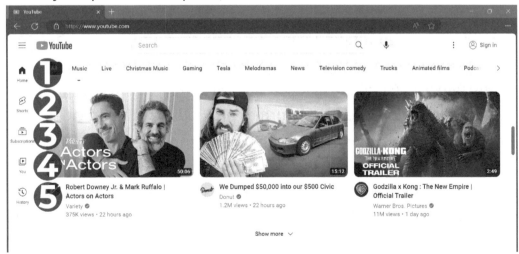

② **Shorts**. In this section, you can view short videos that are currently trending on YouTube.

③ **Subscriptions**. In this section, you will find the latest videos from the channels you are subscribed to. It's a fast way to access new content from your favorite authors.

④ **You**. This section contains your saved videos, videos you've chosen to watch later, and your favorites.

⑤ **History**. This section contains your browsing history.

Search bar

The search bar is at the top of the page. You can use it to search for videos by entering a topic, video title or channel name.

User account

In the upper right corner, you will find your account icon. You can use it to manage your account, check notifications and go to settings.

It may seem unnecessary to create a Google account to use YouTube. But actually, it opens up a lot of possibilities for a more personalized and comfortable experience. Let's find out why you should have a Google account and how it affects your YouTube experience. **You can create a Google account for free.**

Advantages of Google account for YouTube

① **Personalized content.** A Google account allows YouTube to collect information about the videos you view. This helps more accurately select videos that may be of interest to you.

② **Channel subscription.** With an account, you can subscribe to your favorite channels and receive notifications about new videos, which helps you stay up to date.

③ **Playlists.** You can create playlists to save videos for later viewing.

④ **History.** Browsing history allows you to easily return to previously watched videos.

⑤ **Commenting and interaction.** You can comment on videos and participate in discussions.

⑥ **Impact on YouTube recommendations.** YouTube uses your Google account info to recommend videos that match your interests. This makes viewing more interesting and diverse.

What are the benefits of using YouTube via a Google account

If you have no Google account:

- You can view videos but you can't subscribe to channels, create playlists, or make comments.
- Recommendations are based only on general trends and not on your personal preferences.

If you have a Google account:

- You have access to all YouTube features, including subscriptions, comments, playlists and personalized recommendations.
- Browsing history and interaction with other users.

Note

In the next chapter, we will tell you how to create a Google account and how to use it to log in to YouTube. This will allow you to have access to all features of this service.

How to find a video on YouTube?

1. Type in keywords (such as "how to bake an apple pie") in the search bar and press "Enter".
2. Scroll through the list of videos matching your query and choose the ones you like best.

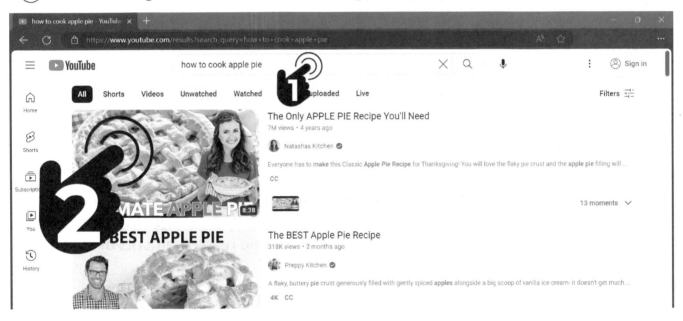

What are YouTube recommendations?

These are videos YouTube finds interesting for you based on your recently viewed videos and interests.

What is a channel on YouTube?

A YouTube channel is a page of a user or organization where all their videos are posted. It's like a personal TV channel for each user.

How to subscribe to a channel on YouTube?

Click on the channel name under the video and then on "Subscribe". This way you will receive updates about new videos from this channel.

YouTube video player

1. **Full screen mode.** Click on the square icon in the lower right corner of the player window. In full screen mode, this icon will minimize the window.

2. **Pause and resume.** Click on a video or press the space bar on your keyboard to pause or resume the video.

3. **Volume.** Use the volume slider in the lower left corner of the window.

4. **Rewind:** Click on the progress bar and move its slider forward or backward.

5. **Next video:** Click on the arrow icon in the lower left corner of the window.

Likes, dislikes and comments on YouTube

You can express your opinion about a video by clicking on the "thumbs up" (like) or "thumbs down" (dislike) icons under the video. You can also comment on videos and read comments of other users.

Tips for finding content

- Use search keywords.
- Browse through various channels to find videos you like.

Examples of search queries on YouTube

- "gardening tips for beginners"
- "overview of new smartphone models"
- "guitar lessons for beginners"

5.5 HOW TO CREATE AND LOGIN TO A GOOGLE ACCOUNT

Imagine you have a magic key that opens the door to many convenient tools and services on the Internet. This key is your Google account. Let's find out why you need one and how to create it.

What is a Google account?

It is an account used to access Gmail, Google Photos, YouTube and many other Google services.

Is it free?

Yes it is. Creating and using a Google account is absolutely free. You will have access to many handy features without any payment.

Google account login

1. **Open a browser.** Click on the browser icon on your computer (for example, the Edge or Chrome).
2. **Go to the Google page.** Type in "**www.google.com**" in the address bar of the browser and press "Enter".
3. **Log in to your account.** In the upper right corner of the page, find and click on the "Sign in" button.
4. Enter login data. Enter your email address or phone number associated with your Google account.
5. Click on the "Next" button and enter your password.

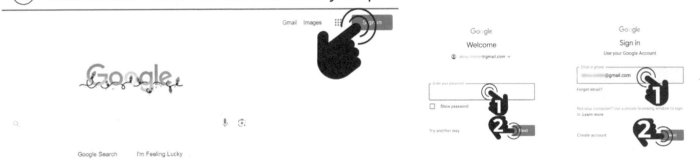

6. Complete login. After entering your password, click on the "Next" or "Done" button.

How to create a Google account (if you don't have one): step-by-step instructions

1. Open the sign in page. Open your browser and type in "create a Google account" in the search bar or go to "accounts.google.com/signup". Or go to www.google.com, click on the "Sign in" and then "Create account" buttons.
2. **Enter your personal data.** You will be asked to enter your first and last name, date of birth, and sex.

(3) Choose your username (this will be your email address) and password.

As a username, you can choose anything you can remember. For example, you can use your first and last name, separating them with a period (spaces are not allowed). You can also add any numbers (year of birth, etc.):

- **linda.hemiltone**
- **john.nash76**
- **lovecraft.alfredo**

How to create a strong password:

(3.1) **Use a combination of symbols.** Your password must include upper and lower case letters, numbers and special symbols, such as !, @, #.

(3.2) **Avoid obvious combinations.** Don't use easy-to-guess combinations like your birthday, pet's name, or "123456".

(3.3) **Use a long enough password.** It must have at least 8 symbols.

(3.4) **Use a unique password.** Don't use the same password for different accounts.

(3.5) After you have created a password, enter it in the "Password" field and enter it again in the "Confirm" field. If you want to see the password you entered instead of ▣▣▣▣▣, check the box "Show password".

(4) **Add a recovery email.** You can use the e-mail address of your trusted relatives. In case of problems, an email for password recovery will be sent to this email address. Enter this email address and click on the "Next" button. If you can not specify such an email, skip this step by clicking on the "Skip" button.

(5) **Add a phone number.** To improve the security of your account, Google may ask you to provide a phone number to verify your identity. To do this, enter your phone number in this field and click on the "Next" button. If you don't have a phone or don't want to enter its number now, click on the "Skip" button.

(6) **Verify the data entered.** If everything is correct, click on the "Next" button.

(7) **Accept the Terms of Use.** Read and accept the Terms of Use. Click on the "I agree" button to continue.

(8) **You're done!** Now you have a Google account! Save the account login and password (login is your email address in the format aaaaa@gmail.com)

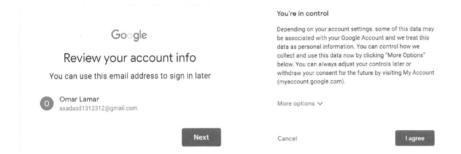

Advantages of a Google account

(1) **Gmail access.** Your account includes free email with a big storage space.

(2) **Synchronization with different devices.** You can sync your account with your phone, tablet, and computer to access your data from any device.

(3) **Access to YouTube and other services.** The account makes it possible to subscribe to YouTube channels, create playlists and interact with other Google services.

(4) **Storage for photos and documents.** Use Google Photos for photos and Google Drive for documents.

(5) **Security and privacy.** Google provides various tools to protect your privacy and data security.

A Google account opens up wide opportunities for comfortable and efficient use of many online services. It is your digital key to the world of information, entertainment and communication. Creating and using a Google account is a step towards a more convenient and organized digital life.

5.6 USING GMAIL

Gmail is a free Google email service. It allows you to send and receive emails, use the calendar, save contacts and much more.

Email is a way of sending and receiving letters over the Internet.

You can send or receive **emails** over the Internet similar to a traditional letter, but much faster.

Generally, the word Email is used both to refer to the email service and what is sent via email. So if you are asked to "write by email" or "send an email", it means the same thing.

Overview of Gmail interface

Imagine Gmail is your mailbox in the digital world. The Gmail interface helps you easily view, send and organize your emails. Don't worry, even if it's your first time, we'll explain everything simply and clearly.

Inbox:

It is your main mail folder, where you will find all the mail you receive. As soon as you open Gmail, you'll be taken there.

Compose:

You can find this button in the upper left corner of your mailbox. It is like a magic key that will help you create a new email.

Navigation panel:

To the left of your mailbox you can find the panel with "Sent", "Drafts", "Spam" and other folders to sort your emails.

Search bar:

It is at the top of your mailbox. You can use it to search for emails, using keywords or addresses.

How to read an incoming email in Gmail?

①   Gmail login. Open a browser, go to the Gmail page (gmail.com), and login to your Google account.

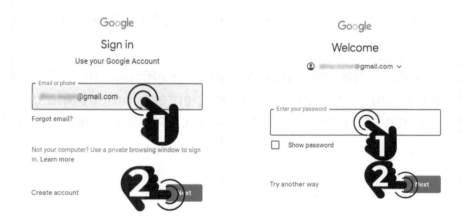

②   **Inbox view:** On the Gmail page, you will see a list of your incoming emails. It is your inbox, where you can view all received emails.

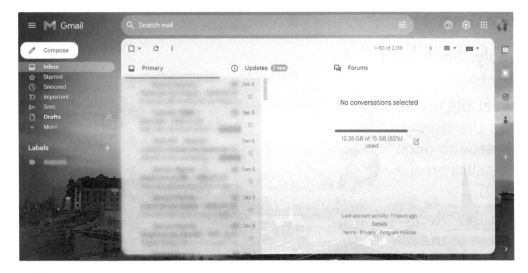

(3) Select an email: Click on any email to open and read it. You will see the name of the sender, the date of sending, the subject of the email, and the text of the email itself.

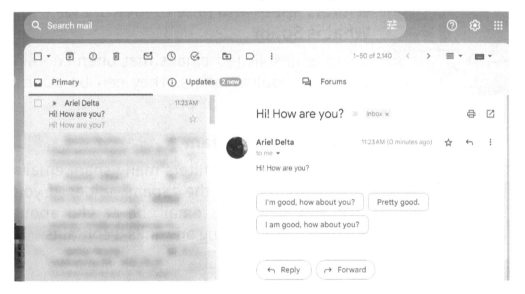

How to create an email in Gmail?

(1) Click on the "Compose" button. On the Gmail page, in the upper left corner, click on the "Compose" button. A new window will open for creating an email.

(2) Enter the receiver's address. In the "To" field, enter the email address of the person you want to send the email to, or start typing the person's first and last name. If the person is in the list of your contacts in the Google account, the address will be entered automatically.

(3) Enter the subject of your email . In the "Subject" field, enter a short description of your email.

(4) Write the text of your email. In the large white box below, enter the text of your email.

(5) Send your email. After writing the text of your email, click on the "Send" button at the bottom of the window.

How to reply to an email in Gmail?

① **Select an email for reply.** Open the email you want to reply to.

② **Reply to an email.** Under the text of the email, you will find the "Reply" button. Click on the button to open the form for reply (1). Or click on one of the reply templates (2).

③ **Write a reply.** Click on the "Reply" button and enter the text of the reply in the form that opens, and then click on the "Send" button to send it.

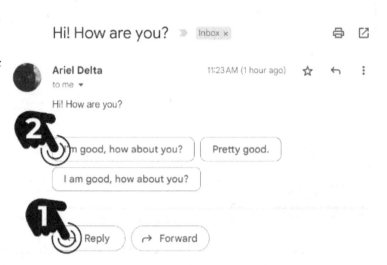

What is Spam and how to identify it?
What is Spam

Spam is unsolicited emails that often contain ads or fraudulent offers. They can be boring and sometimes dangerous.

How to identify Spam

Gmail automatically filters many spam emails by sending them to the "Spam" folder. If you receive a suspicious email, be careful about opening it or following any links it contains.

How to find out your email address

You can find your email address in the upper right corner of the Gmail window after logging your account. Hover the mouse cursor over your account image or click on it with the left mouse button.

Conclusion

Gmail is a very powerful and convenient communication tool today. It makes it possible for you to easily share information, stay in touch with family and friends, and much more. With this knowledge, you're ready to take full advantage of Gmail!

5.7 INTERNET SECURITY BASICS

The Internet is like a big city: it has a lot of interesting things, but you need to know how to protect yourself. Like in real life where we carry our house keys, we need to keep our digital security online.

General recommendations

- **Passwords.** Use strong passwords and do not share them with others.
- **Application updates.** Update your applications and operating system regularly to protect against viruses.

Google search security

Dangerous websites: how to detect and why you should not go to them
Signs of dangerous websites:

(1) **Unusual address.** If a website address looks strange or contains a lot of incomprehensible characters, it is better to stay away. Examples (**don't follow these links**):

   b. *apple.com - applle.com* (**fake name**)

   c. *google.com - gogle.com* (**fake name**)

   d. *amazon.com - bamazon.com* (**fake name**)

   e. *youtube.com - yotube.com* (**fake name**)

   f. *ksdjfkjj11111.hk* (**strange website**)

   g. *azakola3989398hack.com* (**strange website**)

   h. *money.free.3984092fk.com.gov* (**strange website**)

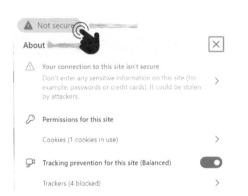

(2) **Browser warnings.** Today browsers often warn about dangerous websites. If you see such a warning, don't ignore it.

(3) **Offers that seem too good.** "Free iPhone just for registration", "Buy a car with a 70% discount!", or "Enter your bank account number and claim your prize!". All these offers seem unreal, don't they?

Why is it dangerous to go to such websites

- You can infect your computer with viruses.
- There is a risk of losing personal data or financial information.

Fake Information. What is fake? How to check information?
What is fake

Fake is false or misleading information. Fakes are created incidentally or on purpose to manipulate you and your opinion about certain things.

How to check information

- **Check a source.** Who is the author of the information? Is this website or media trustworthy?
- **Find confirmation.** Can you find the same information on other reputable and trusted websites?
- **Analyze context.** Is the information used in context, or is it taken out of context to create a sensational headline?

Fighting fakes

- Don't share unverified information.
- Use fact-checking services and tools to verify news.

General advice

- **Critical thinking.** Don't take all information at face value, especially if it causes strong emotions.
- **Safe Internet surfing.** Use reliable antivirus software and update your applications regularly.

Gmail security

Gmail fraud methods

Phishing:

Imagine a situation where you receive an email masked as an official letter from a bank or other reputable organization. In the email, you are asked to provide your personal data or bank details. This is a typical example of phishishing, a fraud method aimed at stealing your confidential information.

Spoofing:

Spoofing is when fraudsters use fake email addresses to pretend to be someone else. For example, you may receive an email that appears to be from your friend. But actually, it is someone else trying to trick you.

Spam:

Spam is unsolicited mail, often with ads or unnecessary information. If you see a strange ad or an email that seems suspicious, it's best to send it to Spam.

Why should you not open files from strangers?

When you open files from strangers, you risk infecting your computer with viruses or malware. This can lead to the loss of important data or even theft of personal information.

Tips for email security

- **Use strong passwords.** Create good passwords and don't use the same password for different accounts.

- **Don't share personal information.** Never provide your personal information in response to suspicious emails.
- **Check emails for authenticity.** If you receive an email from an official organization but have doubts about its authenticity, it's best to verify the information by contacting the organization directly.
- **Update your apps regularly.** Get updates for your antivirus software and browser.

YouTube security

- **Check facts.** Don't take the information from the video at face value. Check the facts with reliable sources.
- Don't share your personal information in video comments.
- If you plan using this service to make and post videos, avoid sharing your personal data. **Don't share your phone number, bank card numbers, home address, etc. in videos.**

How to secure your bank accounts and cards

Don't share your credit card or bank details via email or on suspicious websites. You can also have a separate card for internet spending and subscriptions with a limited budget.

General tips for online safety

- **Antivirus software.** Use reliable antivirus software.
- **Secure Internet connection.** Avoid using public Wi-Fi for important operations.
- **Be careful with links.** Don't click on suspicious links, especially in emails from strangers.
- **Education and awareness.** Update your online safety knowledge from time to time.

5.8 HOW TO USE COPILOT SEARCH

Copilot is your personal assistant in the Internet world. It is like a magical gnome in your computer who helps you find answers to any questions.

Copilot

How to use Copilot in the Edge browser?

1. **Open the Edge browser.** Think of it as a window through which you look at the world.
2. **Click on the Copilot icon.** It's like asking your magical gnome something.
3. Type in a query or use a microphone.

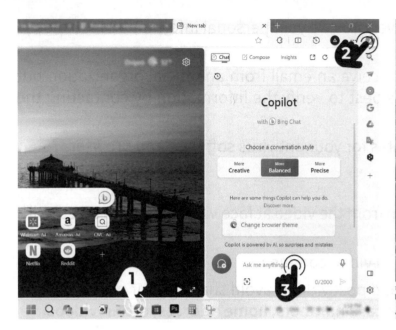

How to use Copilot from the Taskbar

(1) On the Taskbar, find the Copilot icon. Click on it to open the application. It's like starting a conversation with your assistant.

(2) Type in the query that interests you.

If you don't have the Copilot icon on your Taskbar, login in to your Microsoft account and then restart your PC. We will discuss it below.

What are the benefits of Microsoft account

- **If you have an account,** your queries and responses are saved and Copilot "learns" from your previous queries.

- **If you have no account,** you can use Copilot but it won't be able to "remember" your previous queries. Also, Copilot will not be available on the Taskbar.

Overview of Copilot

Imagine that the Copilot window is the control panel of a spaceship. You see a field for your queries, microphone icon, and query templates. Let's take a closer look at the "**Chat**" tab. It is the tab that you will use most often.

What does the conversation style mean?

In Copilot, the conversation style is the way it responds to your queries. For example:

- **Precise.** Copilot responds formally as a teacher.
- **Creative.** Copilot becomes your joking and easy-going companion.
- **Balanced.** Copilot responds not as a teacher but rather like a student.

How to create a query for Copilot?

(1) Open Copilot.

(2) Write what you want to know as if you were writing a letter to an old friend.

Using the microphone for queries

(1) Click on the microphone icon.

(2) Say what you want to know as if you're talking on the phone.

(3) It is important that you have a microphone on your PC. It can be built-in (if it's a laptop) or external (integrated with your headphones or as a separate device).

Sample queries

- Recipes: "Show the borscht recipe".
- Interesting facts: "Tell an interesting fact about space".
- Greeting texts: "Write happy birthday wishes for my friend".

How to start a conversation?

Type in a query or voice it. It's like changing the subject while having tea with a friend. Or click on this button.

How can Copilot help with Windows 11 settings?

Copilot can be your personal assistant in setting up Windows 11. It will provide you with step-by-step instructions and advice.

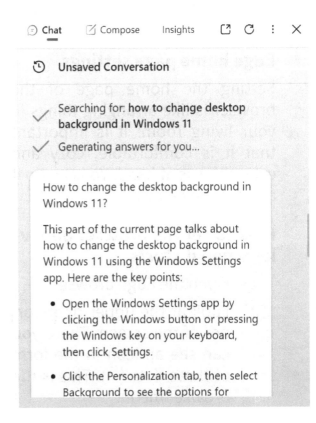

Examples of queries for settings

- **Changing the Desktop background.** "How to change the Desktop background in Windows 11?"
- **Wi-Fi settings.** "How to enable Wi-Fi in Windows 11."
- **System update.** "How to update Windows 11 to the latest version?"
- **Sleep mode settings.** "How to set sleep mode on my computer?"

How can Copilot help with Windows 11 navigation?

Copilot can also be your faithful assistant in understanding how to navigate Windows 11, telling you where important features are and how to use them.

63

Examples of queries for navigation

- **Using the Start menu:** "How to use the "**Start**" in Windows 11?"
- **File management.** "How to find documents in Windows 11?"
- **Screen settings.** "How to change the screen resolution?"
- **Using Microsoft Edge.** "How to use the Edge browser?"

Tips for using Copilot

- **Be specific in your queries.** Clear queries help Copilot better understand what you need.
- **Don't hesitate to experiment.** Try different queries to see how Copilot can help you.
- **Remember that mistakes are normal.** Every query is an opportunity to learn something new.

Conclusion

Using Copilot can significantly simplify your understanding the new operating system. It is like a friendly neighbor, always ready to help. Don't forget that every day is a great opportunity for new discoveries. Good luck learning Windows 11!

5.9 EDGE PERSONALIZATION FOR BEGINNERS

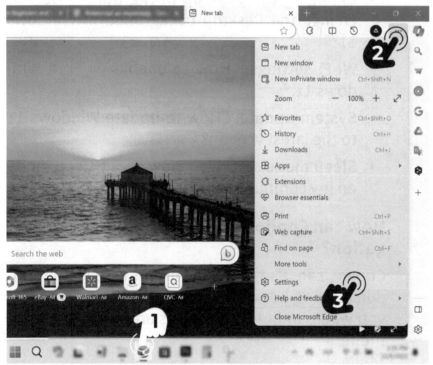

Edge home page settings

Setting the home page of the browser is like arranging things in your living room: it is important that it is comfortable, cozy and everything is at hand. You can do it as describe below.

How to set the browser behavior when it starts

① Open the Edge browser.

② Look at the upper right corner of the screen. There you can see an icon in the form of three dots (⋯). This is the browser menu.

③ Click on the icon and select "Settings" from the drop-down menu.

④ Click on "Start, home, and new tabs".

You will see several options:

① **"Open the new tab page"**. Edge will open a default tab when it starts.

② **"Open tabs from the previous session"**. Edge will restore your last open tabs.

③ **"Open these pages"**. You can enter the URL of your favorite website, such as news or weather. To do this, click on "Add a new page" and enter the address of the website that should open when the browser starts.

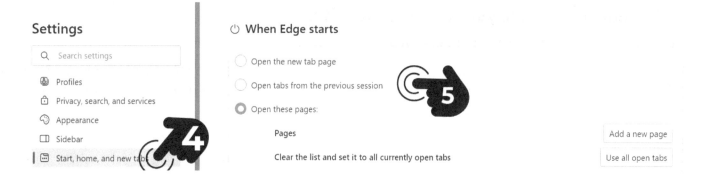

How to set the home page background and layout

① **Go to "Page settings"**. To do it, click on the gear icon on the home page.

② **Home page background**. You can choose a background image from the standard collection or use your own image. To do it, click on "Edit background".

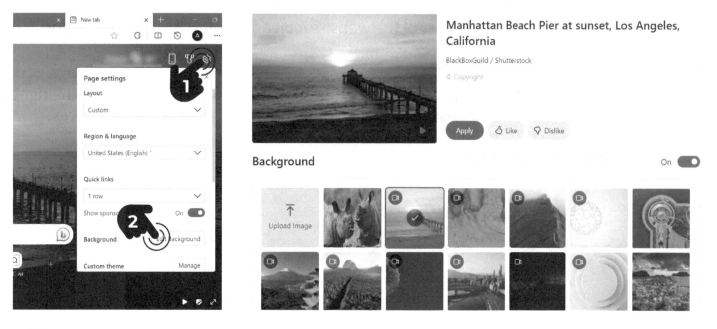

③ **Home page layout**. Choose the layout you like. It can be a focus on the search bar, frequently visited websites, or even an information page with news and weather.

Setting quick access to your favotite websites

(1) On the home page, find "Quick links".

(2) **Add websites.** You can add links to your favorire websites for quick access. It's like adding bookmarks to your favorite book. To do it, click on the "+" sign and enter the address and name of the website.

(3) **Edit or delete websites.** If you want to change or delete the websites you added, click on "..." in the upper right corner of the website icon and select the required option.

Setting the browser color theme

Setting the color theme in the Edge is like choosing colors for your room. Choosing the right theme can make your browsing experience much more pleasant and easy for your eyes.

How to open theme settings

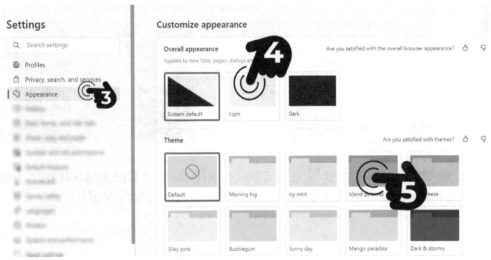

① Click on the icon in the form of three dots (⋯) in the upper right corner of the window.

② Select "**Settings**" from the drop-down menu.

③ Click on "**Appearance**".

④ There you will find the theme settings. You will see three basic theme options and many additional ones:

    a. **Light**. It bright and visually light theme well suited for daytime.

    b. **Dark**. It reduces eye strain, especially in the evening or in low light.

    c. **System**. The browser will automatically select a theme that matches your operating system settings.

⑤ **Other color themes**. Choose the one you like more.

⑥ Select the preferred theme by clicking on the appropriate option.

⑦ The theme will be automatically applied to the browser. You don't need to take any additional steps to activate it.

On this panel, you can also change page scaling in the browser. You can do it this way:

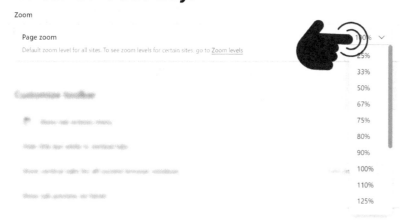

① Scroll down the "**Appearance**" panel to the "**Zoom**" section.

② In the "**Page zoom**" drop-down menu, select the desired page scale.

Testing and feedback

Use the browser with the new theme for some time.

If you feel uncomfortable or just want to change the theme, repeat these steps and choose a different theme.

Edge search settings

Setting the browser search is like choosing a reliable File Explorer in the Internet world. If you opt for Google as your primary search tool, here's how you can set it up in the Edge.

① Open the browser.

② In the upper right corner of the window, find the browser menu icon with three dots (⋯).

③ Click on this icon and select "Settings".

④ On the settings panel, find the "Privacy, search, and services" section.

Address bar and search

Manage search suggestions and search engine used in the address bar

5. In the "Privacy, search, and services" section, click on "Address bar and search".

6. In the "Address bar and search" section, find "Search engine used in the address bar" for search settings.

7. Click on the drop-down meny next to it.

8. Select "Google" from the list of available search engines. If Google is already selected, you don't need to change anything.

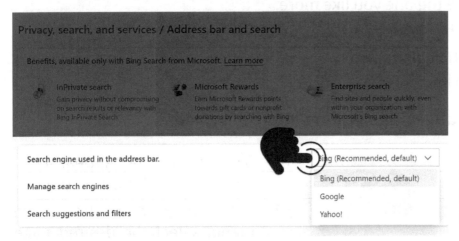

9. After you've selected Google as your search engine, the changes will be saved automatically. You don't need to take any additional steps.

Now, all search queries entered through the browser address bar will be done via the Google Search service.

Chapter 6

USING APPLICATIONS IN WINDOWS 11

In Windows, an application is like a small assistant that specializes in a specific task. It may be an application for writing letters, viewing photos, listening to music, or even keeping accounts. Think of an application as a tool in your digital toolbox.

What applications do you know?

There are many applications you can divide into several categories:

- **Office applications.** These are applications for working with texts, tables, presentations (for example, Microsoft Word, Excel).

- **Multimedia applications.** These are applications for viewing photos, videos, and listening to music (for example, Windows Media Player).

- **Internet browsers.** These are applications for going online (for example, Microsoft Edge).
- **Utility software.** These are applications for setting up and maintaining a computer.
- **Games and entertainment applications.** These are applications for recreation and entertainment.

6.1 OVERVIEW OF BUILT-IN APPLICATIONS

Windows 11 comes with a variety of pre-installed applications that serve essential functions, helping you manage files, browse the web, and more. Below is a detailed overview of these applications, including how to use them and some popular alternatives.

 File Explorer is your primary tool for navigating your computer's files and folders. It allows you to organize, move, copy, and delete files. You can access drives, documents, and cloud storage like OneDrive directly through this app.

How to Use: Open File Explorer from the taskbar or Start menu. Navigate through your folders using the left sidebar. Drag and drop files to move them, or right-click for more options like copy, paste, or delete.

 Microsoft Edge is the default web browser in Windows 11. It's fast, secure, and integrates seamlessly with other Microsoft services. It's also a robust PDF viewer, allowing you to open and annotate PDF files.

Alternative: **Google Chrome and Mozilla Firefox** are popular alternatives. However, Edge's PDF functionality makes it a valuable tool for document viewing and editing.

   Microsoft Office Suite (Web Apps). Windows 11 includes web-based versions of Word, Excel, and PowerPoint, which allow you to create and edit documents, spreadsheets, and presentations online.

How to Use: Access these apps through Microsoft Edge or another web browser by signing into your Microsoft account. Use them for basic document creation and editing.

Alternative: **LibreOffice** is a free, offline alternative offering similar functionality without the need for an internet connection.

  Mail and Calendar. These apps manage your email accounts and calendar events, supporting multiple accounts and syncing across devices.

How to Use: Open the Mail or Calendar app from the Start menu. Add your email accounts by following the prompts. Use Mail to send and receive emails and Calendar to schedule and manage events.

Alternative: Both apps can be replaced with Gmail and Google calendar in the browser.

 Microsoft Store is the central hub for downloading apps, games, and media content on Windows 11.

How to Use: Open the Microsoft Store from the taskbar or Start menu. Browse or search for apps, games, or media, then click "Get" or "Buy" to install them.

Alternative: Some users prefer downloading software directly from developers' websites or using other app stores.

 Photos is the default tool for viewing, organizing, and editing your images.

 Movies & TV plays video files stored on your computer and provides access to purchase or rent movies and TV shows.

How to Use: Open the app, then browse your local videos or use the Microsoft Store to find new content. Play, pause, and skip through your videos using on-screen controls.

Alternative: **VLC Media Player** supports a wider range of video formats and offers more playback options.

 Groove Music plays audio files stored on your device, organizing them into playlists and albums.

Alternative: Spotify for streaming music or Winamp for a feature-rich local music player.

 Snipping Tool lets you capture screenshots of your screen, whether it's a full screen, window, or specific area.

How to Use: Open the Snipping Tool, choose your snip type (Rectangular, Freeform, Window, or Fullscreen), and capture your screenshot. You can annotate and save or share it directly.

 Paint is a simple image editor, perfect for quick edits or drawings.

 Calculator app offers basic, scientific, programmer, and conversion calculators.

 Settings app is the central hub for configuring your Windows 11 system, including personalization, system updates, network settings, and more.

How to Use: Open Settings from the Start menu or by pressing Win + I. Navigate through categories like System, Devices, and Personalization to adjust settings according to your preferences.

 Notepad is a basic text editor, ideal for quick notes or editing simple text files.

How to Use: Open Notepad from the Start menu. Type your text and use the File menu to save or open text files.

Windows 11's built-in apps are designed to cover a broad range of needs, from basic file management to media consumption and beyond. Depending on your preferences, you might find that some third-party alternatives better suit your needs, but these built-in tools provide a solid foundation for everyday tasks.

This list doesn't include applications that may be installed by the computer manufacturer or the ones you can install through the Microsoft Store. Moreover, Microsoft may make changes to the list of pre-installed applications over time.

Installing phone applications on Windows?

It's important to understand that most phone apps are developed specifically for smartphone operating systems like Android or iOS and can't always be installed on Windows. However, some applications have their versions for computers as well, so you can always check the availability of such a version on the official website of the application or in the **Microsoft Store**.

Quick tips and tricks

- **How to find and install a new application**. Use the Microsoft Store, which you'll find on the Taskbar. This is your app store where you can choose and download the applications you want.
- How to uninstall an application. If you no longer need an application, you can delete it by going to "Settings" → "Apps" → "Installed apps". In the list of applications, find the one you want to remove. Next to its name, click on "…" and select "Uninstall". Then follow the instructions of the uninstaller.
- **Application updates**. Regularly check for updates to your apps to use the latest features and maintain security.

We will talk about all this and much more in the following sections of this chapter.

6.2 SOURCES FOR APPLICATIONS

Installing applications is like adding new "helpers" to your computer. It can be an application for processing photos, viewing emails, or even for playing chess.

To install an application on your computer is like inviting a new guest into your home. For everything to go smoothly, you should prepare for it. Here are some tips to help you do that.

1. Application source check

- **What is it?** The app source is where you download the app from. It may be a website, disk, or online store like the Microsoft Store.
- **Why is it important?** Downloading an application from an untrusted source can infect your computer with viruses.
- **What to do?** Download applications from the official websites of the app developers or the Microsoft Store.

2. Windows 11 compatibility check

- **What is it?** Compatibility means that an application will work correctly on your Windows version.

- **Why is it important?** If an application is not compatible with Windows 11, it may not work properly or may not start at all.

- **What to do?** Before downloading, check the information about the application on the developer's website or in the Microsoft Store.

3. Viruses and malware

- **What is it?** Malware can harm your computer or steal your personal data.

- **Why is it important?** Even if the source seems reliable, there is always a risk of downloading malware.

- **What to do?** Use a trusted antivirus program to scan files before installation.

4. System requirements

- **What is it?** These are the minimum or recommended specifications of your computer necessary for the application to work.

- **Why is it important?** If your computer doesn't meet these requirements, the application may run slowly or incorrectly.

- **What to do?** Check the specifications of your computer (you can do it by going to "Settings" → "System" → "About") and compare them with the requirements of the application you want to install.

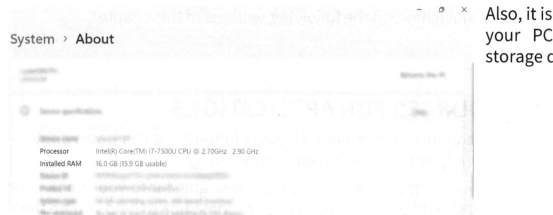

Also, it is very important that your PC has enough free storage drive space.

What is a storage drive?

Imagine that the storage drive in your computer is like a big closet for storing things. Only instead of clothes and dishes, you store digital files there: documents, photos, videos, music and even applications that you install. But just like in a real closet, space in this "digital closet" is limited. So sometimes you should do a "general cleaning" to free up space.

How to find out how much free space is on the storage drive

① Find the "This PC" icon on the Desktop or in the Start menu. If you can not find it there, click on the "File Explorer" icon on the Taskbar. In the Explorer, on the quick access panel, select "This PC".

② There you will see different drives (usually labeled as "Local Disk (C:)", "Local Disk (D:)", etc.).

③ Under the drive icons, you will see information about the used and free space. It's like looking at the shelves in the closet to see how much space is still there.

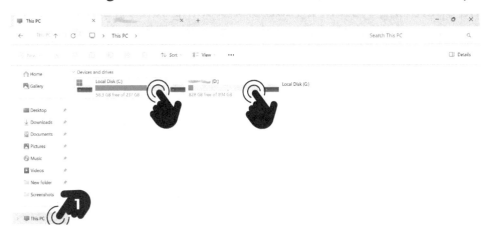

How to free up space on your storage drive

Deleting unnecessary files:

① Browse the files on your computer and delete the ones you no longer need (old documents, photos, applications).

② Use "Recycle Bin" to delete but don't forget to empty it afterwards (right-click on the Recycle Bin icon on the Desktop and select "Empty Recycle Bin").

③ Use drive cleanup apps: Windows 11 has integrated drive cleanup tools that help delete temporary files and other unnecessary data. You can find this tool by opening "**Settings**", going to "**System**" and selecting "**Storage**".

Storage management

🗄 Storage Sense
Automatically free up space, delete temporary files, and manage locally available cloud content

✎ Cleanup recommendations
Storage optimized, no action required

Keeping track of the free space on the storage drive of your computer is very important for several reasons:

- **Preventing computer freezes**. When your storage drive runs out of free space, your computer may start to run slower or freeze. This is because the operating system and applications need additional space for temporary files while they are running.

- **Difficulty saving new files**. If your storage drive runs out of space, you won't be able to save new files or download new applications. This may be a problem, especially if you need to save important documents or other files.

- **Problems with software and operating system updates**. Installing software and operating system updates often requires additional storage drive space. If there is not enough space, updates cannot be completed, which can make your system vulnerable to security risks.

- **Reduced system performance**. Computers often use part of the storage as "virtual memory" to optimize performance. When storage drive space is limited, the efficiency of using virtual memory decreases, which can slow down your computer.

What happens if space runs out?

If there is no free space left on the storage drive:

- Your computer may start to run very slowly and unreliably.

- Downloading and installing new applications will be impossible.

- System and software updates will not be done, which may make your system vulnerable to viruses and other threats.

- You may have problems saving files and performing tasks that require additional storage drive space.

What sources can you use to install applications

You can install applications on your PC in different ways, like choosing where to buy new clothes: from a store, on the Internet, or at the market. Each option has its advantages and disadvantages.

1. Microsoft Store

Microsoft Store is the official app store for Windows 11, which you will find right on your computer.

Pros:

- **Security**. All applications are checked for security, so the risk of downloading malicious software is minimal.

- **Ease of installation**. You can install applications in just a few clicks.

- **Automatic updates**. Applications are updated automatically, so you always have the latest versions.

Cons:

- **Limited selection.** Not all applications are available in the Microsoft Store, so the selection may be limited.

2. Official websites

You can download applications directly from the websites of their developers.

Pros:

- **Large selection.** You can find almost any application there.
- **Latest versions.** Often, the latest versions of applications are available on official websites.

Cons:

- **Security risk.** There is a risk of downloading malware, especially if you visit unofficial or fake websites.

3. Disks

You can buy some applications on physical media such as BD or DVD.

Pros:

- **Offline installation.** Installation is possible without an Internet connection.
- **Physical copying.** You have a physical copy of the application.

Cons:

- **Outdated versions.** The disks may not have the latest versions of the applications.
- **Risk of loss.** If the disk is damaged or lost, you may lose access to the application.

6.3 DOWNLOADING APPLICATIONS FROM THE MICROSOFT STORE

Think of the Microsoft Store as a large supermarket, but instead of goods, it sells applications for your PC. It's a convenient way to add new features and capabilities to your digital device.

How to create a Microsoft account

First, you need a Microsoft account. Creating a Microsoft account is like getting a key to a world of digital possibilities. With its help, you can not only buy applications in the Microsoft Store, but also synchronize data, receive updates and much more.

Step 1. Go to the Microsoft website

1. Open a browser, such as Microsoft Edge or any other browser you use.
2. Go to the Microsoft website. Type in www.microsoft.com in the address bar of the browser, and press "Enter".

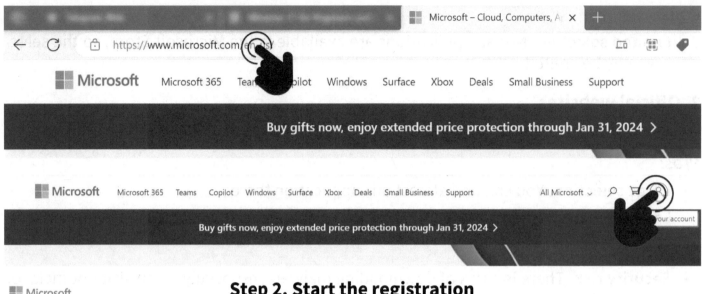

Step 2. Start the registration

1. Find the "Sign in" account authorization button. Usually, it is in the upper right corner of the page.
2. Click on this button to open the authorization form.
3. Next to "No account?" click on "Create one!"

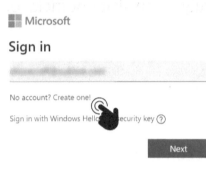

Step 3. Enter your personal data

1. **Enter your email address.** It will be your Microsoft account login username. You can use your Gmail address for it:

    b. *linda.miltone@gmail.com*

    c. *garry.larry@gmail.com*

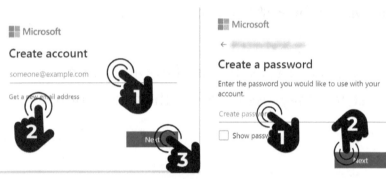

2. **If you don't have an email address,** click on "Get a new email address" and create an email address as described above in the chapter about creating a Google account. Save the email address so you don't forget.
3. Click on "**Next**" to continue.

4. **Create a password.** Create a strong password that is difficult to guess. It must contain letters, numbers and special symbols. (The process is similar to creating the password for a Google account. See the corresponding chapter). Save the email address so you don't forget.

Microsoft

← ▬▬▬▬▬

Verify email

Enter the code we sent to ▬▬▬@gmail.com.
If you didn't get the email, check your junk folder or
try again.

Enter code

☐ I would like information, tips, and offers about
Microsoft products and services.

Ising **Next** means that you agree to the Microsoft Services
Agreement and privacy and cookies statement.

Next

⑤ Click on "**Next**" to continue.

⑥ **Add additional information.** This may include your name, country of residence and date of birth.

⑦ **Pass the security check.** This can be entering symbols from an image or text from a message. If you use the Gmail address as your Microsoft email address, an email with a verification code will come to your Google mail. Go to the Inbox, find the email from Microsoft and copy the code. Then, go back to the Microsoft page and enter this code (1). Click on "I would like…" if you would like to receive information emails from Microsoft (2).

⑧ Click on "**Next**" to continue. (3)

Step 4. Complete the registration

After email verification, your Microsoft account will be created.

Now you can use this account to sign in to the Microsoft Store, as well as other Microsoft services.

How to open the Microsoft Store

Opening the Microsoft Store on your Windows 11 computer is like opening the door to a big store where you can find everything from basic to advanced applications. Let's see how to do it step by step.

Option 1. Find the Microsoft Store icon on the Taskbar

① Usually, you will find the Microsoft Store icon on the **Taskbar** in Windows 11. It looks like a small bag with the Windows logo.

② **If you can't find the Microsoft Store icon** on the Taskbar, go to Option 2. It is especially the case if you've just installed Windows 11 or haven't used the Store before.

Option 2. Open the "Start" menu

① **Click on the icon with the Windows logo.** Generally, this icon is in the lower left corner of the screen.

② **View the list of applications.** In the "Start" menu that opens, you will see a list of available applications and utilities. If you don't see the "Microsoft Store" there, click on the "All apps" button.

③ **Scroll through the list of applications.** Find the Microsoft Store among other applications.

④ **Open the Microsoft Store.** Click on the application icon or name to open it.

77

Option 3. Use the search bar

If you can't find the Microsoft Store through the Start menu:

1. **Use the search bar.** To do it, click on the magnifying glass icon on the Taskbar.

2. Type in "Microsoft Store" in the search bar and select the appropriate application from the search results.

Overview of the Microsoft Store interface

When you first open the Microsoft Store on your Windows 11 PC, you may be surprised by the number of options you can find there. Microsoft Store has a fairly simple and intuitive interface, but let's take a closer look at it.

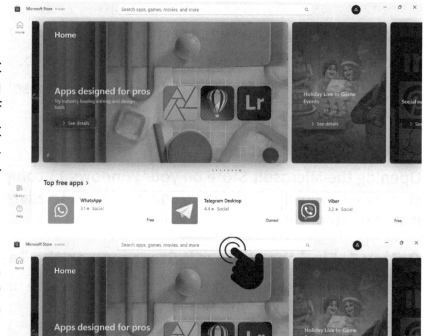

Home page

When you open the Microsoft Store, the first thing you'll see is the home page. It is like a shop window where various goods are on display.

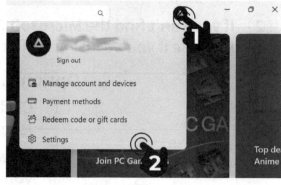

- On the home page you will find **selected sections** such as "Top free apps", "Top free games", "Best selling games" and others.

- You can **scroll down** the page to see more categories and offers.

Microsoft Store search

At the top of the Store page, you will find the **search bar**.

- If you are looking for a specific application or game, enter its name in the search bar.

- Press **Enter** or click on the **magnifying glass** icon to start the search.

My account and settings

In the upper right corner of the screen, you will find your account icon and settings.

- **Your account icon.** Click on it to view and manage your Microsoft account.

- **Settings.** You can also use this icon to access the Store settings, where you can see various options such as payment methods, purchase history and more.

How to install an application (using WhatsApp as an example)

(1) In the Microsoft Store search bar, enter "WhatsApp".

(2) Click on the application in the search results.

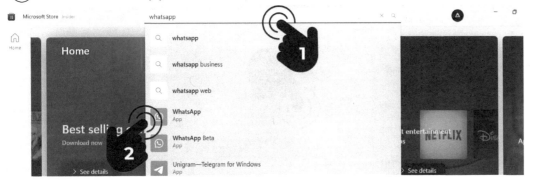

(3) Click on the "Get" or "Install" button to start the download and installation.

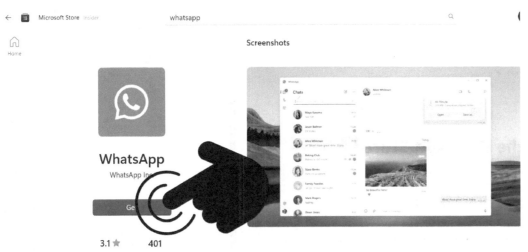

(4) You're done, the application is installed!

How to update Microsoft Store apps?

As a rule, applications you install through the Microsoft Store are updated automatically. You can also check for updates on the download and update page of the Microsoft Store:

(1) On the Microsoft Store sidebar, select "Library".

(2) In the upper right corner of the page, click on the "Get Updates" button.

③ All Microsoft Store apps will be automatically updated.

How to uninstall Microsoft Store apps?

① Go to the "Settings" on your computer.

② Select "Apps", and then "Installed apps".

③ Find the required application in the list and click on "...".

④ Select "Uninstall".

How to buy apps at the Microsoft Store?

① Find the application you want to buy.

② Click on the price or buy button.

③ Enter payment details. (Consult with relatives or friends before buying.)

Microsoft Store is a convenient and safe way to add new applications in Windows 11. You'll easily find what you need there, whether it's free chat apps like WhatsApp or other useful tools. Remember you are always in control of what you install, and you can easily uninstall unnecessary programs. So feel free to go into the world of digital possibilities with the Microsoft Store!

6.4 HOW TO INSTALL APPLICATIONS FROM THE INTERNET IN WINDOWS 11

You can download various applications from text editors to photo albums and games. The Internet offers a wide range of applications for any need.

General safety measures when downloading applications from the Internet

- **Use secure sources.** Download applications from trusted sources. Official developer sites or well-known app stores are your best choice.
- **Avoid suspicious websites.** If a website looks suspicious or offers something for free you would normally pay for, it's best to skip it.

Finding trusted download sources

Check the reviews. You can find a lot of user reviews on the Internet. Use them when choosing a reliable source.

Use official websites. Download applications from the official websites of their developers.

How to download and install applications

Go to the official website. Enter the website address in your browser and go to it.

Find the download page. Usually you can go to it by clicking on the "Download" or "Get" button.

Select the application version. Make sure the selected version is compatible with Windows 11.

Download and install the application. After downloading the application, open it and follow the installation instructions.

Safety tips

- **Be careful.** Avoid downloading applications from unverified sources.
- **Use antivirus updates.** Update your antivirus software regularly to protect against new threats.
- **Stay tuned for Windows updates.** They may contain important security improvements.

Installing applications from the Internet can significantly expand the functionality of your Windows 11 computer. The main thing is to always be careful when choosing download sources and installing applications. This way you will keep your digital space safe and can enjoy new opportunities without unnecessary worries.

6.5 HOW TO DOWNLOAD AND INSTALL AVAST ANTIVIRUS IN WINDOWS 11

Think of an antivirus as a loyal watchdog standing guard over your computer. It is specialized software protecting your computer from various types of malicious software known as "viruses". It not only detects and removes viruses, but also prevents them from getting into the computer.

Why do you need an antivirus application?

- **Malware protection.** Antivirus software helps you avoid getting infected with viruses that can steal your personal data or damage files.
- **Internet security.** Antivirus applications protect while surfing the Internet by blocking malicious websites and downloads.
- **Cyber attack prevention.** Antiviruses can prevent hackers from trying to gain access to your computer.

What is a virus, and what viruses do you know?

Computer viruses are applications designed to cause harm: data theft, file damage, or uncontrolled distribution. There are different types of viruses:

- **Spyware.** These viruses collect your personal data without your knowledge.
- **Adware.** These viruses are used to show unwanted ads.
- **Trojan horses.** These viruses are disguised as legitimate applications but cause harm.
- **Worms.** These viruses spread over the network, damaging systems.

Windows Defender in Windows 11

This antivirus software has these basic features:

- **Automatic scanning.** It regularly scans your computer for malware.
- **Real-time protection.** It blocks malware and files while they are being downloaded.
- **Security updates.** It automatically updates to provide protection against the latest threats.

Should you use another antivirus software?

It depends on your specific needs.

- Windows Defender is often sufficient for **basic protection**. If you don't plan to install additional applications from the Internet and only need a PC for communication, watching news and videos, the basic functionality will be enough for you. You will need no other antivirus software.
- If you often use the Internet or store important information, you may need **advanced protection**. So you should use some other antivirus software with more features.

Since we are now advanced users and plan to use the Internet, we will consider installing third-party antivirus software, for example, Avast Antivirus, namely, its free version.

Installing antivirus software is like putting on a protective helmet before riding a bicycle. In this section, we'll take a closer look at how to download and install Avast Antivirus to keep your computer safe.

How to install Avast

Step 1. Go to the Avast official website

1. **Open Microsoft Edge.**

② **Go to the Avast official website.** In the browser address bar, type www.avast.com and press "Enter".

Step 2. Select the Avast version

① **View available options.** On the Avast website, you will find different antivirus versions, including free and paid options.

② **Select the required version.** For most users, the free version offers sufficient protection.

Step 3. Download Avast

① **Click on the download button.** Select "Free download" or the corresponding button for another version of your choice.

② **Save the file to your computer.** When prompted, select "**Save as**" or "**Open**" in the browser pop-up window. In our case, click on the "**Open**" button.

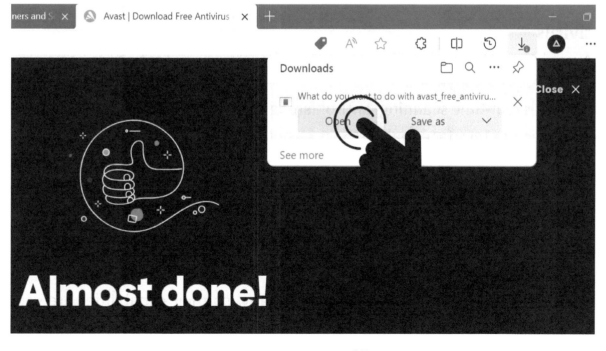

Step 4. Install Avast

(1) **Allow the antivirus to make changes.** If the "User Account Control" window opens, click on "Yes".

(2) **Follow the installer instructions.** The Avast installer will guide you through the installation process. You can choose a standard installation or customize the installation options. In our case, it is enough to choose a standard installation.

Step 5. Complete the installation

(1) **Wait for the installation to complete.** This may take a few minutes.

(2) **Restart the computer.** This will ensure the correct operation of the antivirus.

Step 6. Test and update Avast

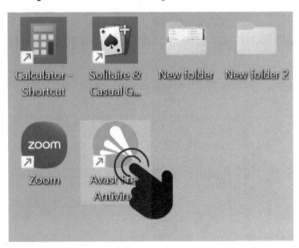

(1) **Start Avast.** After restarting the computer, find the Avast icon on the Desktop or in the Start menu and start it. If the application starts, everything is fine and its installation has been completed correctly.

(2) **No need to check for updates.** Antiviruses update their database automatically, if the Internet is available.

You're done! Now you are protected from most troubles on the Internet.

Still be careful. As they say, better safe than sorry, so don't lose vigilance. Antivirus software doesn't protect against fraudsters, so don't share your confidential information (such as credit card numbers, your credentials, address, etc.) with strangers.

Finally, let's see what other antivirus applications are available.

Avast Free Antivirus

- **What is it?** Avast is one of the most popular antivirus applications that offers basic protection against viruses and spyware.
- **Features.** It includes real-time scanning, anti-phishing and network security.
- **Ease of use.** The simple interface makes Avast easy to use even for users who are not tech-savvy.

AVG AntiVirus Free

- **What is it?** AVG is another popular free antivirus that offers comprehensive protection.
- **Features.** In addition to antivirus protection, it includes features to improve performance and privacy.
- **Note.** AVG and Avast are products of the same company, so their capabilities are very similar.

Bitdefender Antivirus Free

- **What is it?** Bitdefender is known for its powerful lightweight protection technologies.
- **Features.** It offers automatic scanning and detection of sophisticated threats.
- **Potential users.** It is perfect for those looking for a "set it and forget it" type of antivirus.

Microsoft Defender

- **What is it?** It is a solid option for basic protection.
- **Features.** Protection against viruses, spyware, and other types of malware.
- **Ease of use.** It is integrated directly into Windows 11, so it does not require additional installation.

Selection criteria

Use these criteria when choosing an antivirus application:

- **Protection level.** Does the application sufficiently protect against various types of threats?
- **System impact.** Some antiviruses can slow down older computers.
- **Convenience of the interface.** Are you comfortable using the application interface?

When choosing an antivirus application, you not only protect your computer but also your peace of mind. Even using free versions, you can significantly increase the security of your digital activity. But surely, it is important to remember that even the best antivirus is not a reason to ignore the basic rules of safe behavior on the Internet.

6.6 HOW TO INSTALL ZOOM

ZOOM is like a magical portal that allows you to see and communicate with people from all over the world through your computer. This video conferencing application allows you to get together with family, friends, colleagues, even if you are in different parts of the world.

Before installing Zoom on your PC or laptop, there are a few key points to consider:

- **Webcam.** A webcam is required for other members to see you. Most laptops today have built-in web cameras. If you have a desktop computer, you may need an external webcam.
- **Microphone.** For you to be heard during the meeting, you need a microphone. Many laptops have built-in microphones, but desktop PCs may require an external microphone or headset.
- **Speakers or a headset.** You will need speakers or a headset to hear other participants. Although most laptops have built-in speakers, using a headset can improve sound quality and reduce outside noise.

- **Fast enough processor.** Although Zoom does not require a particularly powerful processor, older computers may have problems processing the video.

How to download Zoom

(1) **Open a browser.** Open a browser on your computer. You can use Microsoft Edge, Google Chrome or another browser.

(2) **Visit the Zoom website.** In the browser address bar, type **www.zoom.us** and press "Enter".

(3) **Download the application.** Find the "**Download**" section at the very bottom of the home page of the Zoom website.

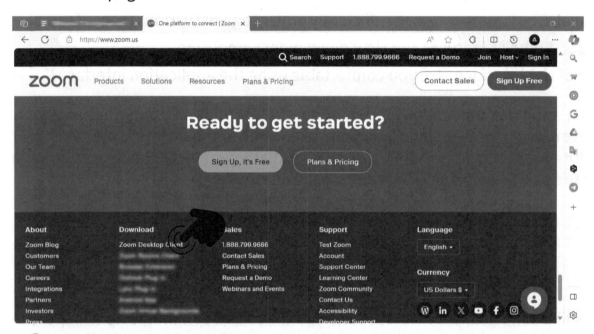

(4) **Select "Zoom Desktop Client"** and click on the "**Download**" button.

Zoom Desktop Client

Phone, Meetings, Chat, Whiteboard and more for your desktop.

The web browser client will download automatically when you start or join your first Zoom meeting, and is also available for manual download here.

Download .10 (26186) (64-bit)

Download 32-bit Client Download ARM Client

Install Zoom

(1) **Open the installer file.** In the pop-up window, click on the "**Open**" button to immediately open the file. Or click on the "**Save As**" button to save the file to install the application later. To do it, after the download is complete, find the file in the "**Download**" folder on your computer. Double-click on the file to start the installation.

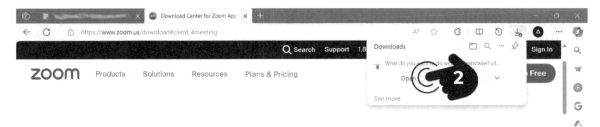

(2) **Installation**. If prompted to allow changes to your device, click on "**Yes**".

(3) Follow the on-screen instructions to complete the installation.

Open Zoom

(1) **Find the Zoom icon.** After installation, the Zoom icon will appear on your Desktop or in the "Start" menu.

(2) Start the application. Click on this icon to open Zoom if the application doesn't open after installation.

Zoom welcome screen

You will see 3 buttons on the welcome screen of Zoom:

(1) **Join a Meeting.** Use this button to join an existing meeting. Then, enter the code of this meeting (you can get the code from the one who created the meeting) and your name.

(2) **Sign Up.** Use the button to create a Zoom account. We will not use it.

(3) **Sign In.** Use the button for Zoom authorization.

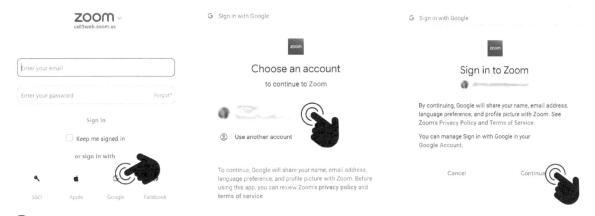

(1) In the window that opens, click on the "**G**" icon to login to Zoom using your Google account. Or you can use your Apple account, if you have one.

(2) Google account authorization page will open. On the page, click on the image of your account. If you have no Google account, you should create it. See the previous chapters of this book to know how to do it.

③ Google will offer you additional information about the use of your data. Click on the "**Continue**" button.

④ Then a pop-up window "**Always allow...**" appears at the top of the browser. Check it and click on the "**Open**" button.

Zoom home screen

After opening Zoom, you'll see the home screen that looks like this:

Big buttons in the center of the home screen:

① "**New meeting**". Use the button to start a new video conference.

② "**Join**". Use the button to join an existing meeting.

③ "**Schedule**". Use the button to schedule a meeting for a specific time.

④ "**Share screen**". Use the button to share your screen.

Menus at the top of the screen:

⑤ "**Team Chat**". You can use this menu to discuss various topics with other Zoom users.

⑥ "**Meetings**". You can use this menu to view your scheduled meetings.

⑦ "**Contacts**". You can use this menu to see a list of people you can chat with via Zoom.

Settings in the upper right corner of the screen:

Click on your account icon in the upper right corner and select "**Settings**".

Audio and video settings

Zoom audio settings are like setting your TV and radio for better signal reception. This is important so you can clearly hear others and be clearly visible during video conferences. Here's how you can do it.

Audio settings

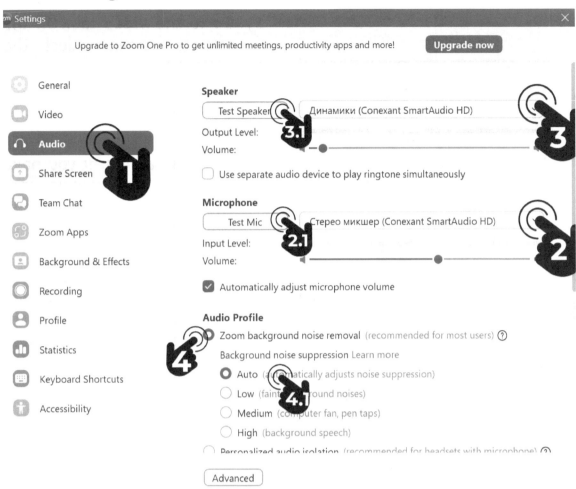

① **Go to the Audio tab.** On the settings screen, select the "**Audio**" tab.

② **Test microphone.** In the "**Microphone**" section, select your microphone from the list. If you only have one microphone (as in the case of laptops with built-in microphones), you don't need to select anything.

(2.1) Click on the "**Test Mic**" button to see if you can be heard clearly. To do this, say something. The "**Input Level**" slide should move from left to right.

③ **Test speakers.** In the "**Speaker**" section, select your speakers or headset. If you only have one speaker or a headset, you don't need to select anything.

(3.1) Click on the "**Test Speaker**" button to make sure you can hear other participants.

④ **Select an audio profile.** Check "**Zoom background noise removal**". It is necessary for Zoom to filter your microphone sound. Then the other meeting participants will hear no background noises from your computer or air conditioner.

(4.1) It is recommended to set the noise removal level to "Auto". Then Zoom will automatically measure the noise level and reduce it. If noises are still heard or your voice sound is too low, select a different level of noise cancellation.

Video settings

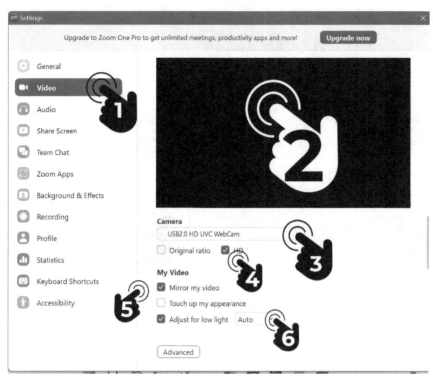

(1) **Go to the Video tab.** On the settings screen, select the "**Video**" tab.

(2) **Camera preview.** Here you will see a preview of the video from your webcam.

(3) **Select a camera.** If you have more than one camera connected, you can select the required one from the list of available cameras.

(4) **Select video quality.** Check the box "**HD**" for the image from your webcam to be in high quality. For this, you must have fast Internet access.

(5) **Select to mirror your image.** To do it, check the box "**Mirror my video**".

(6) **Select to automatically improve video quality in low light**. Check the box "**Adjust for low lights**" and select "**Auto**".

Video image settings:

You can adjust the brightness and other video image settings if your camera and software support it.

Advanced Background & Effects settings

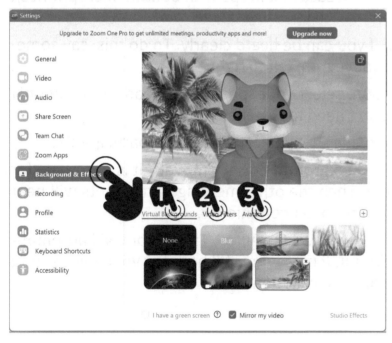

(1) **Virtual background.** On the "**Background & Effects**" tab, you can also select a virtual background that will replace your real background with an image or video.

(2) **Video filters.** On the "**Video filters**" tab, select the filter you like. To disable filters, select "**None**".

(3) **Avatars.** On the "Avatars" tab, you can select an animal that will replace your image in the video and repeat your movements. You shouldn't do this, because this option will make you not serious.

Video settings Create a meeting in Zoom

New Meeting   Join

(1) Start Zoom on your computer or go to the home screen of the application.

(2) **Click on the "New meeting" button** on the home screen of Zoom.

(3) **Select the meeting settings.** When prompted to allow network access to this application, select "Yes".

(4) **Audio settings.** Then check the box "**Automatically join audio..**" and click on the "**Join with Computer Audio" button**. This is required to always create and join meetings with audio. Otherwise, no one will hear you.

(5) **Invite participants.** On the meeting screen, click in the upper right corner of the "**Participants**" tab to get the meeting invite link. Copy and send the link in any way convenient for you to another person or people. (To do this, in the field where you enter text, for example in Whatsapp, right-click and select "**Paste**" and send the message).

How to join a Zoom meeting

Via a link:

If you have a link to a Zoom meeting, click on it. Zoom will automatically open and you will join the meeting.

Via a meeting ID:

(1) Start Zoom and click on the "**Join**" button.

(2) Enter the meeting ID you received.

(3) Enter your name to be displayed during the meeting.

(4) Enter the meeting password if required. Otherwise, click on the "**Join**" button.

New Meeting

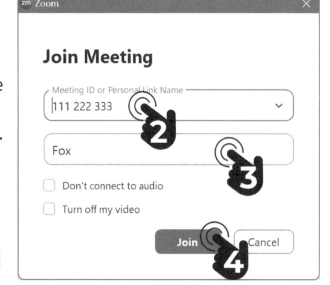

Overview of a Zoom meeting interface

The Zoom meeting interface is like a remote control that lets you control your virtual meeting. It has various buttons and functions that make communication more convenient.

Video of participants

On the screen you see videos of other meeting participants. If someone doesn't have video enabled, you'll see their name or account image.

Control panel

Usually, this panel is at the bottom of the screen. You will find various buttons and options to manage the meeting on it.

Control buttons

1. **"Mute"**. Use the button to turn your microphone on or off.
2. **"Video"**. Use the button to turn your camera on or off.
3. **"Participants"**. Use the button to view the list of meeting participants.
4. **"Share screen"**. Use the button to share your screen or a specific window on your computer.

All other menu buttons are not important for meetings, so we will not focus on them.

How to end a Zoom meeting

1. **"End" button**. To end or leave a meeting, click on the "**End**" button. The button is usually in the lower right corner of the control panel.

2. **Option selection.** If you are the one who created the meeting, you will be asked to choose between "**End meeting for all**" and "**Leave meeting**" options. If you choose the first second option, you will end the meeting for all, and if you choose the second option, you will only leave it yourself, while others will continue to communicate.

6.7. INSTALLING ADVANCED SOFTWARE AND GAMES

After mastering basic tasks, you may want to explore more advanced software that requires a powerful PC or laptop. While we're not diving into how to become an expert in Photoshop or professional video editing, it's important to understand if your computer can handle these programs.

Understanding System Requirements

Most advanced software comes with system requirements detailing what kind of hardware is needed. These typically include the CPU (processor), GPU (graphics card), RAM (memory), and disk space. You can find these requirements on the official website where you're downloading the software or by searching "[program name] system requirements" online.

To compare these requirements with your PC or laptop's specs:

1. **Check Your System Specs:**

    b. *Windows Settings: Open the Start Menu, go to "Settings," then "System," and select "About." This will show your device's specifications, including the processor, RAM, and system type.*

    c. *Task Manager: Right-click on the taskbar and select "Task Manager." Under the "Performance" tab, you'll see detailed information about your CPU, memory, disk, and more.*

2. **Compare Specs with Requirements:** Compare the specs of your computer with the software's system requirements. If your computer meets or exceeds the recommended specifications, it should run the software smoothly. If it only meets the minimum requirements, the software may run, but it might not perform well.

Installing and Running Games

The term "gaming laptop" or "gaming PC" can be misleading because different games require different levels of performance. High-end games may need powerful GPUs and CPUs, while others might run fine on less powerful hardware.

- **Minimum vs. Recommended Requirements:** Games typically list both minimum and recommended system requirements. The minimum requirements are the bare minimum your computer needs to run the game, but it might not run smoothly. The recommended requirements suggest what's needed for the best experience.

- **Where to Download Games:** The two most popular places to download games are:

    c. *Microsoft Store: Pre-installed on Windows 11, offering a variety of games, including casual and some more advanced titles.*

    d. *Steam: A popular platform for downloading and managing games. It has a vast library of titles ranging from indie games to high-performance AAA games.*

By understanding system requirements and checking your computer's specifications, you can make informed decisions about installing advanced software and games, ensuring a smooth and enjoyable experience.

Essential Apps for Work

When it comes to work-related tasks, everyone has unique requirements, making it impossible to create a one-size-fits-all list of essential apps. However, there are some common file types that most professionals will encounter and need to open, edit, or create. These include:

- **.docx** (Word documents): Used for text files, reports, letters, and written content.

- **.xlsx** (Excel spreadsheets): Utilized for data organization, financial records, and calculations.
- **.pdf** (Portable Document Format): Used for sharing documents that are formatted to be read-only, but can still be edited with certain tools like Adobe Acrobat.
- **.png, .jpeg** (Image formats): Commonly used for images in reports, presentations, or websites.

Recommended Apps for Viewing and Editing

- **Microsoft Office** (Word, Excel, PowerPoint): Ideal for editing and creating .docx, .xlsx, and presentation files (.pptx). These programs are industry standards for many types of professional work.
- **LibreOffice:** A free alternative to Microsoft Office, supporting most Office file types, such as .docx and .xlsx.
- **Google Docs/Sheets/Slides:** Cloud-based alternatives for creating and editing Word and Excel files.
- **Adobe Acrobat:** The go-to software for viewing, editing, and creating PDFs. While PDF files are designed to be uneditable, Acrobat allows users to modify them if necessary.
- **Edge/Chrome:** Both browsers offer built-in PDF viewers for easy reading.
- **GIMP** and **photopea.com:** Free image editing software that works well with .png and .jpeg files, offering more control than basic image viewers.

Where to install applications

Typically, modern computers come with more than one storage drive, such as a fast SSD for the system and an HDD for larger storage. Windows will often prompt you to choose where to install the program when installing software. If your system has multiple drives, deciding which drive is best for the app's performance and storage needs is essential. In this section, you'll learn how to make informed choices based on your available storage options and the type of application you're installing.

Scenario 1: One SSD

If you have a single SSD in your system, it's straightforward: all apps should be installed on this SSD. SSDs are much faster than traditional hard drives, so installing apps here ensures they load and run quickly. With only one drive, you don't need to worry about managing where apps are stored.

Recommendation: Install all apps on your SSD for the best performance.

Scenario 2: Two SSDs (One for System, One for Storage)

In a setup where you have two SSDs—one for the operating system and one for storage—the best approach is to install critical apps, like the operating system, system utilities, and frequently used software on the primary SSD (where Windows 11 is installed). This keeps them fast and responsive. Your secondary SSD can be used for apps that require more space, such as games or large programs.

Recommendation:

- **Primary SSD (System):** Install essential software, operating system, and high-performance apps.
- **Secondary SSD (Storage):** Install games, media apps, or large programs that you don't need to run at top speed all the time.

Scenario 3: SSD for System (1TB) and HDD for Storage

If your setup includes a large SSD (1TB or more) for your operating system and a traditional HDD for storage, you should prioritize installing important and performance-sensitive apps on the SSD. The HDD is slower and better suited for files like documents, photos, videos, and backup data, rather than apps that need to run quickly.

Recommendation:

- **SSD:** Install the operating system and all apps that benefit from fast loading times, such as games, media-editing software, or any programs you use frequently.
- **HDD:** Use for storing large files, backups, and any non-critical apps that don't require high performance.

Chapter 7

USING EXTERNAL DEVICES IN WINDOWS 11

Think of external devices as special tools that can be connected to your computer for different purposes, like magic keys that unlock new possibilities. Let's take a closer look at what they are and how to use them.

What is an external device?

An **external device** is any device or additional equipment you connect to your computer through a port (for example, a USB port). These include a printer for printing documents, a scanner for scanning photos, or an external drive for storing a large number of files.

How to connect external devices to a PC?

(1) **Finding a port.** First, find a vacant port on your computer where the device will be connected.

(2) **Connection.** Take the cable of the external device and connect it to the port. Most devices today are connected via a USB port.

What is a USB port, and what types of USB ports do you know?

- **USB** (Universal Serial Bus) is a universal port for connecting many types of devices. There are different types of USB ports, including:
- **USB 2.0.** It is an older version suitable for most devices. But it has a lower data transfer rate.
- **USB 3.0.** It is a newer and faster version. Its connector is often blue on the inside.
- **USB-C.** It is the latest version characterized by a smaller connector and high data transfer speed.

What external devices do you know?

- **External drives,** such as hard drives and flash drives for data storage.
- Printers and scanners, for printing and scanning documents and photos.
- **Multimedia devices,** such as webcams, smartphones, microphones and headphones for communication on the Internet.
- **Input/Output devices,** such as keyboards and mice for more efficient PC control.

7.1 CONNECTING EXTERNAL DEVICES

Imagine your computer is your digital home and external devices are your guests. In this section, you will learn how to "invite" these various devices to your Windows 11 home.

Connection options

- **Wired connection.** It's like connecting an electric kettle. You should just plug the device's cable into the appropriate port on your computer.
- **Bluetooth.** It is a wireless connection option similar to using a remote control. Enable Bluetooth on your computer and the device, then follow the on-screen instructions to pair them.
- **Radio connection.** Use a special radio module that plugs into a computer's USB port to connect devices like a wireless keyboard or mouse.

How to connect a keyboard to a PC

Wire keyboard connection

- **Select a USB port on your PC.** Use any port that matches the USB type of the keyboard's cable.
- **Connect the keyboard.** Plug the keyboard's USB cable into the selected USB port.
- **Check connection.** After connection, Windows 11 will automatically detect the new device. If the keyboard doesn't work, try reinserting the cable into the port or using a different port.
- **Keyboard interaction.** Start using the keyboard to type or navigate your computer.

Wireless keyboard connection

1. **Insert the USB receiver.** Take the USB receiver that comes with the keyboard and plug it into a USB port on your PC.

2. **Turn on the keyboard.** Turn on the keyboard using the power switch, if present.

3. **Pair the keyboard with the PC.** Most wireless keyboards automatically pair with a PC when turned on. If the keyboard doesn't pair automatically, check the manufacturer's instructions for manual pairing.

4. **Check and use.** After connecting the keyboard, try to type text or use the keys to test it.

How to connect a mouse to a PC
Wire mouse connection

1. **Select a USB port on your PC.** Any free USB port will do.

2. **Connect the mouse.** Plug the mouse's USB cable into the port.

3. **Check connection.** The cursor will appear on the screen when you move the mouse. If the mouse doesn't work, try another port.

Wireless mouse connection

1. **Insert the USB receiver.** Connect the receiver that comes with the mouse to the USB port.

2. **Turn on the mouse.**

3. **Pair the mouse with the PC.** Most wireless mice automatically pair with a PC. If the mouse doesn't pair, check the manufacturer's instructions.

How to connect a microphone to PC and laptop
Wire microphone connection

1. **Find the audio port.** It is a pink port, or the one marked with a microphone icon.

2. **Connect the microphone.** Insert the microphone connector into the appropriate port.

3. **Check the microphone.** Right-click on the sound icon in the tray and select "Sound settings". Make sure the microphone is selected as the default device.

USB microphone connection

1. **Connect the microphone to a USB port.** Plug the USB cable of the microphone into a USB port on the computer.

2. **Microphone settings.** Go to "Sound settings" to select the microphone as the default recording device.

How to connect headphones to a PC and laptop

(1) **Headphones with a 3.5 mm (mini-jack) connector.** Plug them into the audio port (usually green).

(2) **Bluetooth headphones.** Enable Bluetooth on the headphones and the PC, and then pair them.

How to connect a webcam to PC

(1) **Select a USB port.** Find a free USB port on your computer.

(2) **Connect the webcam.** Plug the webcam's USB cable into the selected port.

(3) **Check connection.** The computer will automatically detect the camera. You can test the camera by opening any application that uses the camera (such as Skype or Zoom).

(4) **Camera settings.** In the settings of the application where you use the camera, select your webcam as the default device.

How to connect a flash drive to a PC and laptop

(1) **Select a USB port.** Find a free USB port on your computer.

(2) **Connect the flash drive to the port.**

(3) **Check connection.** The computer automatically detects the flash drive. If it is not displayed, try a different port.

(4) **Data access.** Go to "This PC" or "File Explorer" -> "This PC" to view the contents of this flash drive.

How to connect an external hard drive to a PC and laptop

(1) **Connect the drive.** Using a USB cable, connect the external hard drive to a USB port.

(2) **Check connection.** After connecting the hard drive, the computer will detect it. If the drive isn't displayed, make sure it's turned on and try a different USB port.

(3) **Data access.** Go to "This PC" or "File Explorer" -> "This PC" to view the contents of this hard drive.

How to connect a printer and scanner to a PC and laptop

(1) **Connect a printer/scanner to a PC** using a USB cable.

(2) For wireless devices, turn them on and set up a Wi-Fi or Bluetooth connection.

③ Install drivers. Some devices may require drivers to be installed. Follow the instructions that come with the device or on the manufacturer's official website.

④ **Check and use.** Check the connection by opening "Bluetooth & devices" in the "Settings" menu. There you will find the item "Printers & scanner" where the name of your printer should be displayed.

⑤ Try printing a test page or scanning according to the printer's instructions. To do this, select any text document, click on it with the right mouse button and select "**Print**".

How to connect Bluetooth devices in Windows 11?

In Windows 11, Bluetooth is like using a radio to communicate between different devices without the need for wires. Here's how you can establish a wireless connection between your computer and other devices, such as headphones or a mouse.

Step-by-step instructions

Make sure your computer supports Bluetooth. Most modern PC and laptops have built-in Bluetooth.

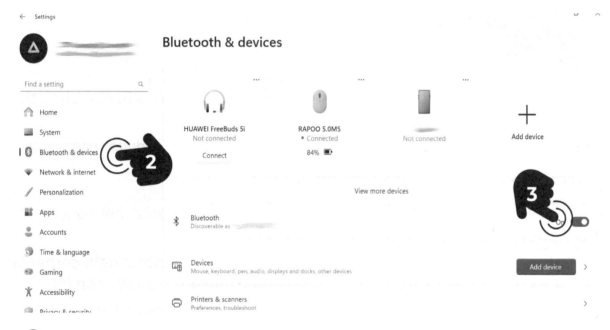

① **Turn on Bluetooth on the computer.** Right-click the Windows icon in the lower left corner of the screen and select "Settings".

② In the "**Bluetooth & devices**" section, find "**Bluetooth**".

③ Turn the switch to the "**On**" position.

④ Turn on Bluetooth on the device you want to connect.

⑤ Make sure your device is in pairing mode (see the manufacturer's instructions for your device).

Pairing devices

(1) In the "**Bluetooth & devices**" section, click "**Add a device**".

(2) Select "**Bluetooth**" and wait for your computer to find your device.

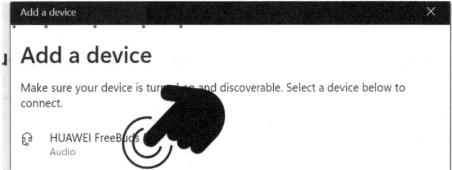

(3) Select your device from the list and follow the on-screen instructions to complete the pairing.

(4) **Check connection.** After successful pairing, the device should be ready for use.

How to Connect to a Wi-Fi Network in Windows 11

Connecting to Wi-Fi in Windows 11 is like tuning your computer to a wireless network for internet access. Here's how you can easily connect to a Wi-Fi network.

(1) **Open Wi-Fi Settings:** Click on the Wi-Fi icon in the taskbar at the bottom right corner of your screen. If you don't see the icon, it might be hidden under the arrow icon (^).

(2) **View Available Networks:** A list of available Wi-Fi networks will appear. Ensure Wi-Fi is turned on by checking that the Wi-Fi button is highlighted.

(3) **Select Your Network:** Find your Wi-Fi network name (SSID) from the list and click on it.

(4) **Connect to the Network:** Click "Connect" after selecting your network. If the network is secured, you'll be prompted to enter the Wi-Fi password.

(5) **Enter Password:** Type the password and click "Next". Windows will connect to the network and save the password for future use.

(6) **Check Connection:** Once connected, you'll see "Connected, secured" under your network's name. You can now access the internet.

What are drivers?

Driver is a special application that helps your computer "talk" to hardware or external devices. It's like a translator between your PC and your device.

Are drivers updated automatically and how to update them?

Update drivers automatically

1. Drivers are usually automatically updated through Windows Update.
2. To check for updates, go to Settings > Windows Update.
3. Click "**Check for updates**" to download and install any available driver updates.

Download from the manufacturer's website

1. Visit the website of your hardware manufacturer.
2. Find the support or download section and select the required drivers.
3. Download and install the drivers by following the instructions.

Understanding how to connect Bluetooth devices and update drivers is an important part of using Windows 11. It will help ensure that your devices work properly and that your computer remains safe and efficient.

All of these external devices add new features to your computing experience, making it more productive and convenient. Knowing how to connect and use these devices is key to working efficiently with your computer whether it's printing important documents, storing large amounts of data, or simply using a flash drive to transfer photos.

7.2 CONNECTING MOBILE DEVICES

Connecting a mobile phone to a computer or laptop is like building a bridge between two islands: this connection allows you to transfer data such as photos, music, and documents.

How to connect an Android device to a PC

① **Use a USB cable.** Take the USB cable that comes with your Android device. Connect one end of the cable to your phone and the other to a USB port on your computer.

② **Select a connection mode.** On the phone, a request to select a connection mode may appear on the display or the Notification Center (this is where you receive all messages, at the top of the display). Select "**File transfer**" or "**Media transfer (MTP)**".

③ **Data transfer.** On the computer, open File Explorer, where you'll find your device and view its contents as if it were a folder on your computer.

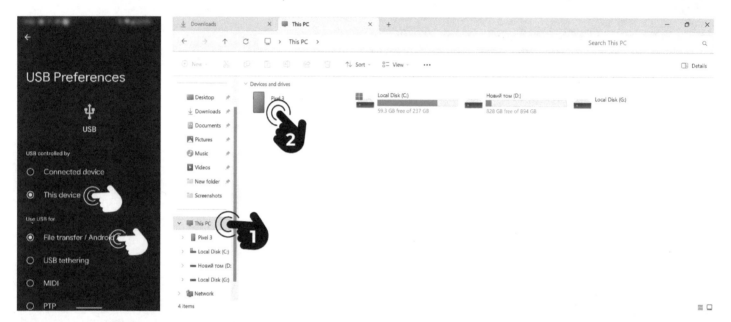

How to connect an iOS device to a PC

Connection via USB cable

① **Find a suitable USB cable.** Use the cable that came with your iOS device. Usually, it is a cable with a Lightning connector (for older devices) or a Type-c connector (for newer models).

② Connect one end of the cable to a port on your iOS device.

③ Connect the other end of the cable to a free USB port on your computer.

④ You may be prompted to allow access to data on your device. Confirm this.

How to copy photos from a smartphone to a PC

① **Connect the smartphone to the PC** using the above methods, depending on the type of your smartphone.

② **Open the photo folder.** On the computer, open "File Explorer" and find the folder with photos on your smartphone.

③ **Copy the photos.** Select the photos you want and copy them to a folder on your computer, in the same way as copying ordinary files and folders.

How to move photos from a PC to a smartphone
① **Connect the smartphone to the PC** using a USB cable.
② **Open the folder on the computer.** Find the photos you want to transfer.
③ **Copy the photos.** Copy the selected photos from the folder on your computer and paste them into the corresponding folder on your smartphone, in the same way as copying ordinary files and folders.

Viewing and editing photos on a PC
Viewing and editing photos on your Windows 11 computer can be as exciting as going through an old family album and adding your own touches. Let's see how to do this using the built-in Windows tools.

Viewing photos
① **Open photos.** Using "File Explorer" on your PC, open the folder where your photos are stored.
② Double-click on a photo to open it.

Editing photos in the Windows "Photos" application
① **Open photos for editing.** Open the photo you want to edit by double-clicking on it with the left mouse button.

(2) **Crop photos.** Click on the "**Edit image**" icon in the upper left corner.

(3) **Select "Crop".** Cropping frames will appear on the screen. You can move and resize them to select the desired area of the photo.

(4) After selecting the required area, click "**Save options**".

(5) **Change the photo tilt.** In "Crop" mode, you can also change the tilt of the photo using the rotation slider.

(6) Move the slider to tilt the photo in the required direction.

(7) After selecting the required tilt, click "**Save options**".

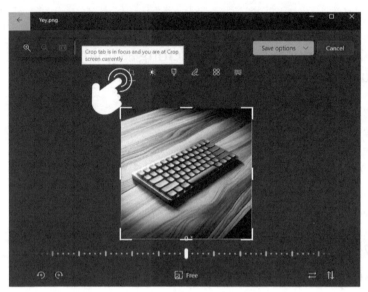 

(1) **Add a filter.** Select "**Filter tab**".

(2) Select one of the available filters to change the look of your photo. (2). You will see the changes immediately in the window on the left.

(3) Also, you can select "**Auto Enhance**" to improve the image automatically. Don't hesitate to experiment.

(4) After selecting the filter, click "**Save options**".

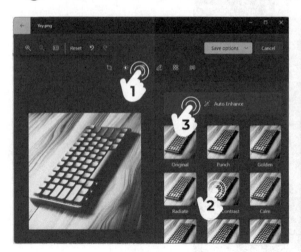 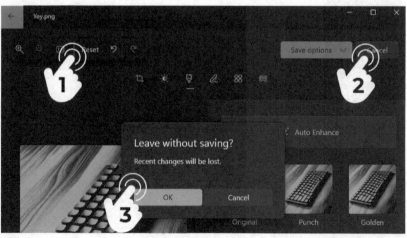

To cancel all changes, click "**Reset**" (1) and continue editing (you can also click the back arrow, which cancels your last action). To leave without saving changes, click "**Cancel**" (2) and select "Ok" (3).

After editing the photo, do not forget to save the changes. You can save the changes to the same file or save the edited version as a new file to keep the original image unchanged.

7.3 TROUBLESHOOTING CONNECTION ISSUES

Connecting external devices to your Windows 11 computer is generally straightforward, but occasionally, you might run into issues. Here are some common problems and how to troubleshoot them:

1. Device Not Recognized

- **Check Connections:** Ensure all cables are securely plugged in. For wireless devices, verify that they are powered on and within range.
- **Try a Different Port:** If using USB, try plugging the device into a different port.
- **Restart Your Computer:** Sometimes, a simple restart can resolve recognition issues.

2. Driver Issues

- **Update Drivers:** Go to Device Manager by right-clicking the Start button and selecting "Device Manager." Find your device, right-click on it, and select "Update driver." Choose to search automatically for updated driver software.
- **Reinstall Drivers:** If updating doesn't work, try uninstalling the device from Device Manager and then restarting your computer. Windows will attempt to reinstall the drivers automatically.

3. Bluetooth Devices Not Pairing

- **Ensure Bluetooth is On:** Double-check that Bluetooth is enabled on your computer.
- **Remove and Re-Pair:** Go to "Settings" > "Bluetooth & devices." Remove the problematic device and try pairing it again.
- **Check Device Compatibility:** Make sure your device is compatible with Windows 11.

4. Wi-Fi Connection Issues

- **Check Wi-Fi Status:** Ensure Wi-Fi is turned on and you are within range of the network.
- **Forget and Reconnect:** Go to "Settings" > "Network & Internet" > "Wi-Fi," click on your network, and select "Forget." Then reconnect to the network by selecting it from the list and entering the password again.
- **Reset Network Settings:** If issues persist, go to "Settings" > "Network & Internet" > "Advanced network settings," and click "Network reset" to restore network settings to default.

5. Printer Not Responding

- **Check Printer Status:** Ensure the printer is powered on and connected to the computer or network.
- **Run Troubleshooter:** Go to "Settings" > "Devices" > "Printers & scanners," select your printer, and click "Run the troubleshooter."
- **Reinstall Printer:** If the problem persists, remove the printer from "Printers & scanners" and add it again.

6. Audio Devices Not Working

- **Check Connections:** Ensure headphones or speakers are properly connected.
- **Set Default Audio Device:** Right-click the sound icon in the taskbar, select "Sound settings," and choose the correct output device.
- **Run Audio Troubleshooter:** In "Sound settings," scroll down to "Advanced" and click "Troubleshoot common sound problems."

If these steps don't resolve your issue, consider consulting the device's user manual or the manufacturer's website for more specific troubleshooting steps. Additionally, keeping your system and drivers updated can help prevent many common issues.

Chapter 8

SPECIFICS OF USING WINDOWS 11

8.1 KEEPING WINDOWS 11 UPDATED

Regular Windows 11 updates are like regular medical examinations. They help keep your computer "healthy" and "strong". Here are some of the benefits of these updates:

- **Security.** It's like replacing old door locks with new, more reliable ones. Updates help protect your computer from viruses and other threats that are constantly changing, which are similar to sneaky thieves trying to break into your home.
- **Improved performance.** Updates can make your computer run faster and more efficiently like you do after a cup of freshly brewed tea.
- **New features.** From time to time, Microsoft adds new useful and interesting features, like adding new channels to your TV.
- **Bug fixes.** Nothing is perfect, and sometimes there appear bugs in software. Updates help fix them to keep things running smoothly.

Frequency of updates

Windows 11 updates regularly. There are two types of updates:

- **Minor updates.** It's like going shopping every week. They are more frequent, maybe once a month, and deal with bug fixes and security improvements.
- **Major updates.** It's like a big general cleaning at home that you do once a year. They are less often, maybe once or twice a year, and deal with new features and significant changes.

Are updates automatic?

Generally, they are automatic. Your computer will "ask" for permission to install an update when you're less busy. However, you can configure the update as described below so it doesn't interfere with having a cup of tea or watching your favorite shows.

Examples of updates

May 2021 Update. This update improved security and quality. It was like a small improvement of your home interior.

October 2021 Update. This update was more significant, introducing new features such as a new Start menu design and other conveniences. It was like getting a new TV with a higher image resolution and more channels.

Remember that updates are your friends in the tech world. They help keep your computer "fit" and "healthy".

Check for updates

1. Go to "**Settings**".
2. Select "**Windows Update**".
3. Click "**Check for Updates**" to see if there are any updates available for your system.

Download and install updates

1. **Download.** If updates are available, click "**Download and install**".

2. **Installation.** After downloading, the system may prompt you to restart your computer to complete the installation.

Update schedule

As Gandalf from "The Lord of the Rings" would say, the update will be when it is due. You can set the time for automatic updates so it doesn't interfere with your tea time or watching your favorite shows. It's simple! In the settings section, you can select a time that is convenient for you. It's like scheduling a meeting with an old friend.

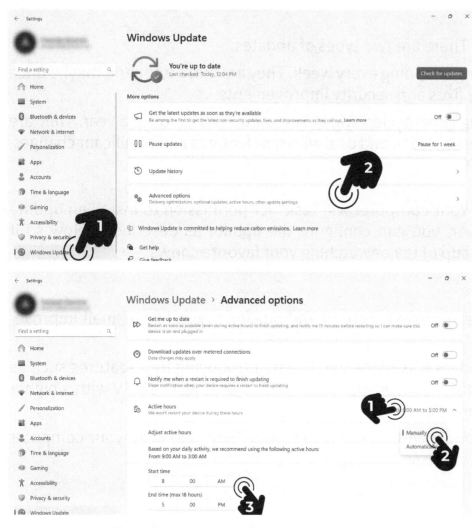

A step-by-step guide to schedule Windows 11 updates is given below.

(1) Go to "**Settings**".

(2) Select "**Windows Update**".

(3) Find "**Advanced options**" where you can set the time for updates.

(4) In "**Advanced options**", select the "**Active hours**" option (1). Then select "**Manual**" (2) and set a specific time when you are working on the PC so updates are not installed at that time (3).

(5) **Save the changes**, once you've chosen a time that is good for you.

Common problems

These can happen during updates. If your computer seems confused during an update, restart it. It's like letting him rest and focus.

Let's take a look at some of the most common problems you may encounter when updating Windows 11 and how to fix them:

Problem: errors when downloading updates

How to solve:

- Check your Internet connection.
- Restart your computer and try downloading the update again.
- Use the Windows Update Troubleshooter available in Settings.

Problem: not enough space for updates

How to solve:

- Delete unnecessary files and apps to free up drive space.
- Use the Disk Cleanup tool for Windows to automatically delete temporary files.
- Move large files to an external drive or cloud storage.

Problem: updates get stuck or freeze

How to solve:

- Restart your computer.
- If the problem persists, use Windows recovery mode.
- In the latter case, try going back to the previous version of Windows.

Problem: errors after the update

How to solve:

- Restart your computer.
- Check system settings and installed drivers.
- If the problem persists, use a system restore point from before the update.

Problem: The computer won't start after the update

How to solve:

- Try starting the computer in safe mode.
- Use Windows recovery tools.
- If all else fails, you may need to reinstall Windows.

Problem: sound or video problems after the update

How to solve:

- Check if the drivers of sound and video cards are updated.
- Restart your computer.
- Use the Windows Sound Troubleshooter.

Problem: Internet connection lost after the update

How to solve:

- Restart your router and computer.
- Check your network settings.
- Update your network adapter drivers.

All of these problems have their solution, and usually you should start with the simplest steps, such as restarting your computer. If this doesn't help, use built-in recovery tools and troubleshooting utilities.

Importance of drivers

Drivers are instructions for your computer hardware. Think of them as recipes for your favorite dish. If the ingredients (drivers) are out of date, the dish may not be good. So, updating drivers helps your hardware work properly.

Update security

As in the movie "Home Alone", it's better to be safe than sorry. When updating, make sure your antivirus is active and up-to-date. It's like having a good dog guarding your home. Also, don't forget to back up important files regularly. It's like keeping a spare house key just in case. Copy the files you don't want to lose to a flash drive or external hard drive. Also, consider using cloud storage services like Google Drive.

8.2 WINDOWS 11 ACTIVATION

Not too long ago, activating Windows was one of the first steps you needed to do when setting up a new computer. However, most PCs and laptops now come with Windows 11 pre-installed and already activated. This makes the process much easier for users. But it's still important to understand what happens if Windows isn't activated, the types of licenses available, and how to activate Windows if necessary.

What Happens If Windows Isn't Activated?

If your copy of Windows 11 isn't activated, you'll see a watermark on your desktop reminding you to activate Windows. You'll also have limited access to personalization options like changing the desktop background, colors, and themes. Despite these limitations, most essential functions will still work, such as browsing the internet, using apps, and running software.

Types of Windows 11 Licenses

1. **OEM (Original Equipment Manufacturer) License:** This is the most common type, pre-installed on new computers. It's tied to the specific hardware of your device, meaning you can't transfer it to another computer.

2. **Retail License:** Bought separately from stores or online, this license can be transferred to another device if you decide to upgrade or replace your computer.

3. **Volume License:** Typically used by businesses, this allows a single key to activate multiple installations of Windows.

How to Activate Windows 11

1. **Check Activation Status:** Open the Start Menu, go to "Settings," then "System," and click on "Activation." Here you can see if your Windows is activated.

2. **Activate with a Product Key:** If you have a product key, click on "Change product key" and enter it. Follow the on-screen instructions to complete activation.

3. **Activate Using a Digital License:** If your device is already associated with a digital license (common with pre-installed systems), Windows 11 should automatically activate as soon as it connects to the internet.

Where to Buy a Product Key

You can purchase a genuine Windows 11 product key from the Microsoft Store, authorized retailers, or online through the official Microsoft website. Avoid buying from unknown sources, as counterfeit keys may not work and can pose security risks.

By ensuring that your Windows 11 is activated, you gain access to all personalization features and regular updates, keeping your system secure and fully functional.

8.3 COMMON PROBLEMS AND THEIR SOLUTIONS IN WINDOWS 11

This section lists the most common problems and general troubleshooting tips.

Since some of the solutions below may be difficult to understand, it is recommended to learn more about how to solve these problems on Copilot or Google. Create queries for these search engines, such as:

- No sound - how to update drivers in Windows 11
- No sound - how to set up in Windows 11

In other words, formulate a query following this pattern: "problem" - "solution option" - "in Windows 11"

1. Problems with starting and loading

Problem: a computer doesn't start or freezes at the start.
Solution: reboot, safe mode, system restore.

2. Internet connection problems

Problem: no Internet or unstable connection.
Solution: checking network settings, restarting the router.

3. Problems with updates

Problem: unable to download or install updates.
Solution: using the update troubleshooter, manually updating.

4. Audio and video problems

Problem: no sound, problems with video playback.
Solution: updating drivers, sound settings.

5. Problems with login and accounts

Problem: unable to log in, account problems.
Solution: password recovery, new account creation.

6. Speed and performance problems

Problem: slow system operation, application freezes.
Solution: disk cleanup, application startup management.

7. Software problems

Problem: applications won't open or work incorrectly.
Solution: reinstalling applications, using compatible mode.

8. Problems with external devices

Problem: problems with connecting printers, scanners, external devices.
Solution: checking the connection, updating drivers.

9. Problems connecting to the printer

Problem: a printer doesn't print.
Solution: checking the printer connection, updating the printer drivers, restarting the printer and the computer.

10. Problems with the display

Problem: incorrect display resolution or image quality problems.
Solution: adjusting the display resolution in the settings, updating the video card drivers.

11. Sound problems

Problem: No sound or sound quality issues.
Solution: checking sound settings, the connection of audio devices, updating audio drivers.

12. Security problems

Problem: suspicious security notifications or suspected viruses.
Solution: scanning for viruses, updating the antivirus program, using Windows security tools.

13. Problems with Wi-Fi

Problem: interrupted Wi-Fi connection or low speed.
Solution: restarting the Wi-Fi router, checking the Wi-Fi settings, updating the drivers of the network adapter.

14. Problems with logging the system

Problem: problems signing in with a Microsoft account.
Solution: resetting the account password, checking the Internet connection settings.

15. Problems with data storage

Problem: out of drive space or storage error.
Solution: using disk cleanup tools, checking the drive for errors.

16. Accessibility problems

Problem: problems with the use of the system by persons with disabilities.

Solution: setting up accessibility features in Windows, such as increasing fonts, voice input.

17. Bluetooth problems

Problem: unable to connect to Bluetooth devices.
Solution: checking Bluetooth settings, restarting Bluetooth devices, updating Bluetooth drivers.

18. Problems with displaying applications

Problem: applications are not displayed correctly on the screen.
Solution: changing display zoom settings, checking application compatibility.

19. Problems with the file system

Problem: errors when reading or writing files.
Solution: checking the drive for errors, using the CHKDSK utility to repair the file system.

20. Problems installing applications

Problem: nable to install new applications.
Solution: check for free drive space, run installation as administrator, check security settings.

21. Problems with file recovery

Problem: lost or accidentally deleted files.
Solution: using file recovery tools, checking the recycle bin for deleted files.

22. Power management problems

Problem: a computer suddenly shuts down or enters sleep mode.
Solution: adjusting energy saving options, checking system power settings.

23. Problems with fonts

Problem: incorrect display of fonts in applications and web browsers.
Solution: installing and updating fonts, resetting font settings in the browser.

24. Problems with sound recording

Problem: problems with recording sound through the microphone.
Solution: checking microphone settings, updating audio drivers, checking the microphone connection.

25. Problems with virtual memory

Problem: slow operation of the system due to lack of RAM.
Solution: adjusting the size of virtual memory, optimizing the use of resources.

26. Problems with the touch screen

Problem: the touch screen doesn't respond or works incorrectly.
Solution: restarting the device, checking touch screen settings, updating touch screen drivers.

27. Problems with network folders

Problem: Unable to access shared network folders.
Solution: check network settings, checking folder access permissions, restarting network services.

28. USB speed problems

Problem: low USB data transfer speed.
Solution: using USB 3.0 ports, updating USB drivers, checking for conflicts in the device manager.

29. Problems with system stability

Problem: frequent system crashes or "blue screens of death" (BSOD).
Solution: checking the Windows event log to find the cause of the crashes, checking the system for viruses, updating the system and drivers.

30. Problems with the laptop touchpad

Problem: the touchpad doesn't work or works incorrectly.
Solution: checking touchpad settings, updating touchpad drivers, checking the physical condition of the touchpad.

31. Problems with function keys

Problem: function keys (F1-F12) don't work.
Solution: checking keyboard settings in BIOS/UEFI, updating keyboard drivers, checking keyboard software.

32. Problems with graphics cards

Problem: graphics problems such as screen flickering or incorrect color rendering.
Solution: updating graphics card drivers, checking graphics settings, using diagnostic tools from the manufacturer of the graphics card.

33. Problems accessing Windows Update

Problem: unable to get updates through Windows Update.
Solution: using the Windows Update Troubleshooter, resetting Windows Update components, checking for viruses.

34. Problems with changing the language

Problem: unable to change the language of the interface.
Solution: adding and setting the required language, restart after changing the language.

35. Problems with the scanner

Problem: unable to scan documents.
Solution: checking the scanner connection, updating the scanner drivers, using the Windows Scan application.

36. Problems with sound settings

Problem: resetting sound settings after restart.
Solution: saving sound settings as default, checking for application conflicts.

37. Problems with the task scheduler

Problem: scheduled tasks are not executed.
Solution: checking the task scheduler settings, checking access rights, using User Account Control.

38. Problems with the graphic editor

Problem: graphic editors don't work properly.
Solution: updating graphic drivers, checking the compatibility of the editor with Windows 11, configuring the video card.

39. Problems with autorun applications

Problem: applications don't start automatically at system startup.
Solution: adding application to autorun through settings or registry editor, checking privacy settings.

40. Problems accessing files

Problem: errors accessing certain files or folders.
Solution: checking file access rights, using the "Restore Ownership" command, checking for viruses.

41. Problems with email

Problem: email applications don't send or receive emails.
Solution: check incoming/outgoing mail server settings, check Internet connection, updating email applications.

42. Split screen problems

Problem: unable to use the split screen function.
Solution: check multitasking settings, checking the compatibility of application window modes.

43. Problems with themes

Problem: errors changing the theme.
Solution: updating or reinstalling themes, check theme compatibility with Windows 11, reset settings to default values.

44. Media playback problems

Problem: unable to play certain media files.
Solution: installing the necessary codecs, using alternative media players, checking the compatibility of file formats.

45. Problems with fonts in the browser

Problem: fonts are displayed incorrectly in the web browser.
Solution: clearing the browser cache, checking font settings in the browser, reinstalling the browser.

46. Problems with time synchronization

Problem: the system time is not synchronized automatically.
Solution: using the time synchronization function in the settings, checking the time zone, manually setting the time.

47. Volume problems

Problem: unable to change the volume or it changes by itself.
Solution: checking audio system settings, updating audio drivers, checking sound scheme settings.

48. Problems with Remote Desktop

Problem: unable to connect via Remote Desktop.
Solution: checking firewall settings, checking remote access permissions, checking network settings.

49. Problems with notifications

Problem: system notifications don't appear or appear too often.
Solution: setting up the action center, checking notification settings, restarting notification services.

50. CPU temperature problems

Problem: CPU overheating or high temperature during use.
Solution: checking the cooling system, using applications for temperature monitoring, reducing the load on the processor.

8.4 HOTKEYS IN WINDOWS 11

These are keyboard combinations for specific commands or actions in the operating system or applications. Hotkeys can speed up the work on your computer significantly, allowing you to do various tasks without having to use a mouse or navigate through menus.

What are the benefits?

- **Efficiency.** Hotkeys provide quick access to various functions, allowing you to save time.
- **Convenience.** They help reduce the amount of physical movement, for example, between the keyboard and the mouse.
- **Productivity.** Using hotkeys increases your productivity because you can complete routine tasks faster.

How to use them?

- **Remembering.** First, you should remember some basic hotkeys, such as Ctrl + C for copying and Ctrl + V for pasting.
- **Practice.** Use these keyboard combinations in your daily work. It may seem awkward at first, but you'll get used to it over time.
- **Study.** Learn about additional hotkeys that are specific to apps you use frequently.
- **Setting.** In some applications, you can configure your own hotkeys for even more efficient work.

Basic hotkeys in Windows 11

Hotkeys	Description
Alt + Tab	Switch between open applications and windows. It's like turning the pages of a book.
Windows + D	Show or hide the Desktop. It's like quickly clearing everything from the table.
Windows + E	Open the file manager. It's like opening the cabinet where all your files are stored.
Windows + L	Lock the computer. It's like locking the door when you leave your house.
Ctrl + C	Copy selected text or object. It's like making an exact copy of the key.
Ctrl + V	Paste the copied text or object. It's like inserting a duplicate key into another door.
Ctrl + Z	Cancel the last action. It's like going one step back.
Ctrl + X	Cut the selected text or object. It's like cutting a picture out of paper.
Windows + I	Open settings. It's like opening the manual for the device.
Windows + S	Search. It's like asking something from a smart book.
Windows + V	View the clipboard. It's like going through all the previously copied things.

Hotkeys	Description
Alt + F4	Close the active window or application. It's like closing the book you're reading.
Windows + Print Screen	Take a screenshot of the entire screen and save it. It's like taking a picture of everything you see in front of you.
Ctrl + Alt + Delete	Open the security screen. It's like pressing a special button to call for help.
Windows + A	Open the notification center. It's like looking at a bulletin board.
Windows + M	Minimize all windows. It's like removing all the books from the table at once.
Windows + Shift + S	Take a screenshot of the selected area of the screen. It's like cutting out part of a picture.
Ctrl + Shift + Esc	Open the task manager. It's like seeing a list of all your to-dos.
Windows + G	Open the game panel. It's like getting a special tool for games.
Windows + K	Open the connection panel. It's like searching for available devices to connect.
Windows + L	Lock the computer. It's like locking your book with a key.
Windows + P	Select the display mode for the second screen or projector. It's like choosing where to send a picture.
Ctrl + A	Select all. It's like pointing to all objects in a folder or document.
Ctrl + F	Search in the document. It's like quickly finding the right word in a book.
Windows + T	Switch between applications on the Taskbar. It's like browsing through all the open "books" on the shelf.
Windows + (+)	Enable the magnifier to scale part of the screen. It's like taking a magnifying glass to see small details.
Alt + Enter	Open the properties of the selected object. It's like viewing detailed information about a file or folder.
Windows + Space	Change the input language or keyboard layout. It's like changing the writing tool.

See more hotkeys at: https://support.microsoft.com/en-us/windows/keyboard-shortcuts-in-windows-dcc61a57-8ff0-cffe-9796-cb9706c75eec

Using hotkeys in your daily computer use can greatly increase your efficiency and make your computer experience more enjoyable and productive

8.5 PERFORMANCE OPTIMIZATION AND ADDITIONAL SECURITY IN WINDOWS 11

Performance Optimization

Windows 11 is designed to offer a smooth and efficient experience, but over time, your PC may start to slow down. This could be due to background apps using too many system resources like CPU, GPU, or RAM. Here's how you can check your computer's performance and optimize it.

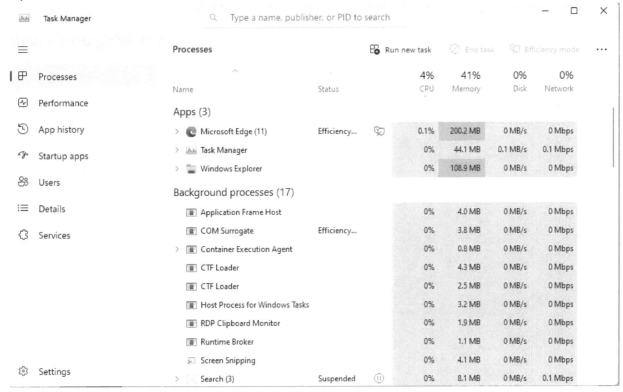

1. **Using Task Manager:** To check which apps are using the most resources, open **Task Manager** by pressing **Ctrl + Shift + Esc**.

   b. *Click on the Performance tab to see the usage of your CPU, Memory (RAM), Disk, and GPU.*

   c. *In the Processes tab, you'll see a list of all running applications and how much CPU, memory, and disk space they are using. If an app is taking up too many resources and slowing down your PC, consider closing it by selecting it and clicking End Task.*

2. **Check Background Apps:** Some apps run in the background even when you're not using them. These can take up system resources unnecessarily. If your computer feels slow, go through the list in Task Manager and close any apps that are not essential.

3. **Uninstall Unnecessary Programs:** If there are programs you don't use, uninstalling them can free up system resources and disk space. Go to **Settings > Apps > Installed apps** to remove unused applications.

④ **Managing Startup Apps:** Some apps automatically launch when you start your computer, using resources unnecessarily. Disabling these can improve performance.

- **How to Enable or Disable Startup Apps:**

  e. Press ***Ctrl + Shift + Esc*** *to open Task Manager.*

  f. *Go to the **Startup** tab.*

  g. *You'll see a list of apps that launch at startup. Right-click on any app and select **Disable** to prevent it from starting automatically.*

  h. *To re-enable an app, return to the list and select **Enable**.*

By managing startup apps, you can prevent unnecessary programs from slowing down your computer right from the start.

Additional Security: Password Managers and Two-Factor Authentication

Security is crucial when using any device, especially as personal data becomes more valuable. While antivirus software and secure passwords are essential, using a **password manager** and **two-factor authentication (2FA)** can take your security to the next level.

① **Password Managers:** Password managers help securely store your passwords for different websites and services. Instead of remembering multiple complex passwords, you only need to remember one master password, and the password manager will take care of the rest. They also generate strong passwords for you.

Why Password Managers Are Better Than Browser Built-Ins:

- **Centralized Security:** Standalone password managers offer encryption and centralized storage, ensuring that even if one browser is compromised, your passwords are still safe.

- **Cross-Platform Access:** Password managers sync your passwords across different devices and browsers, whereas browser-based managers only work within that specific browser.

- **Added Features:** Password managers often include features like secure note storage, breach alerts, and password audits, which are usually lacking in built-in browser tools.

② **Two-Factor Authentication (2FA):** 2FA adds an extra layer of security beyond just passwords. When you log into a website or service, 2FA requires a second form of identification—usually a code sent to your phone or generated by an app—before access is granted.

  c. *How It Works: After entering your password, you'll be prompted to enter a 6-digit code sent to your phone via SMS or generated by a 2FA app like Google Authenticator.*

  d. *Why It's Important: Even if someone steals your password, they won't be able to access your account without the 2FA code, making your accounts much more secure.*

Recommended Password Managers

Here are some reliable password managers, both free and paid:

- **1Password** (Paid): Known for its user-friendly interface and advanced security features, it offers family plans and cross-platform support.
- **LastPass** (Free and Paid): A popular choice, offering a free version with basic features and a premium version with advanced features.
- **Bitwarden** (Free and Paid): One of the best free options, providing robust security and cross-platform syncing.
- **ProtonMail** (Free and Paid): While primarily an email service, ProtonMail offers encrypted services and security solutions that integrate with password management.

Using a password manager combined with two-factor authentication provides strong protection against unauthorized access, helping ensure that your personal information stays safe.

By optimizing your computer's performance and bolstering security with password managers and 2FA, you can enjoy a smoother, more secure computing experience.

EPILOGUE

Dear, reader

First, let me express my sincere gratitude to you for choosing our book. Your decision to expand your knowledge and skills is a great step in the world of today's technology.

Congratulations on reading the book to the end! This is truly an impressive achievement, especially considering how much new information you learned. Your dedication and diligence in your studies deserve special praise.

I hope this book was not only a useful guide for you in learning the basics of Windows 11, but also helped you feel more confident when working with your computer. We tried to make the material as accessible and understandable as possible, so you can easily introduce new knowledge into your daily computer use.

Before you close this book, I would like to give you some advice for your further self-study. These are as follows:

- **Practice.** The best way to consolidate new knowledge is practice. Don't hesitate to experiment with Windows 11 settings and features.
- **Update.** Technologies develop very quickly. Follow software updates and news in the world of technology.
- **Communication.** Join communities, forums, or groups where you can ask questions and share experiences with other Windows users.
- **Educational resources.** Don't stop there. There are many online courses, video tutorials that can help you expand your knowledge.

Remember that learning is a continuous process, and each new step in this direction opens new horizons of possibilities. I wish you the best of luck in your journey into the world of Windows 11 and hope that your efforts bring you joy and satisfaction in using your computer.

Best regards,
ARCHER FOX

Made in United States
Troutdale, OR
12/09/2024